Bob Bertolino, PhD
Kevin Thompson, MEd

The Residential Youth Care Worker in Action
A Collaborative, Competency-Based Approach

Pre-publication
REVIEWS,
COMMENTARIES,
EVALUATIONS . . .

"**F**rom assessment to team meetings, Bertolino and Thompson have given residential youth care workers a gift that will renew their interest in therapy and keep them persevering for change with youth and their parents. The authors' clear and simplified manner of writing respects the importance of RYCWs in residential treatment and their impact in guiding youth toward their goals. The book shows how to learn the essentials of solution-focused therapy and to implement them immediately in every daily procedure in the residential context, creating opportunities for more effective therapy, interaction, treatment planning, discharge planning, and relationship building. Instead of thinking that 'this youth just does not want to change,' the RYCW who reads this book will be motivated to find new ways of making a connection with a youthful client by thinking 'this youth is temporarily off track . . . how can I approach him so that he finds the way back on his own?'

If you work with youths at a residential treatment center, or as a youth leader, therapist, or school-teacher and desire a new approach that will enliven your work, motivate your clients, and increase your success with troubled youth, this book is the resource that will help you to accomplish what you once thought was impossible."

Linda Metcalf, PhD
Author of *Counseling Toward Solutions,*
Parenting Toward Solutions,
Teaching Toward Solutions
and *Solution-Focused Group Therapy,*
Arlington, Texas

The Residential Youth Care Worker in Action

A Collaborative, Competency-Based Approach

HAWORTH Marriage and the Family
Terry S. Trepper, PhD
Executive Editor

The Residential
Youth Care Worker
in Action
A Collaborative,
Competency-Based Approach

Bob Bertolino, PhD
Kevin Thompson, MEd

The Haworth Mental Health Press
New York • London • Oxford

Published by

The Haworth Mental Health Press, an imprint of The Haworth Press, Inc., 10 Alice Street, Binghamton, NY 13904-1580

Cover design by Jennifer M. Gaska.

The Library of Congress has cataloged the hardcover edition of this book as:

Bertolino, Bob. 1965-
    The residential youth care worker in action : a collaborative, competency-based approach / Robert Bertolino, Kevin Thompson.
        p.   cm.
    Includes bibliographical references and index.
    ISBN 0-7890-0701-0 (alk. paper)
    1. Child care workers—Training of—United States. 2. Group homes for children—United States. 3. Group homes for youth—United States. I. Thompson, Kevin, 1966-   . II. Title.
HV863.B47   1999
362.73′068′3—DC21   (ISBN: 0-7890-0912-9)   99-15066
                                                                                              CIP

ISBN 0-7890-0912-9 (pbk.)

To the staff at Youth In Need, Inc., for teaching me well. And, in particular, Laura Harrison, for giving me my first job in the field and for always supporting me.—B. B.

To Justine, my wife and my everything, this is "for you."—K. T.

ABOUT THE AUTHORS

Bob Bertolino, PhD, is an Educational Support Counselor for the Francis Howell School in St. Charles, Missouri. He is also the former Director of Family Court Services at Youth In Need, Inc., founder of Therapeutic Collaborations Consultation and Training, and Adjunct Assistant Professor of counseling and family therapy at St. Louis University, the University of Missouri-St. Louis, and Lindenwood University. Dr. Bertolino has authored or co-authored five books including *Therapy with Troubled Teenagers: Rewriting Young Lives in Progress* and *Even from a Broken Web: Brief, Respectful, Solution-Oriented Therapy for Sexual Abuse and Trauma.* He teaches national workshops on solution-based and collaborative, competency-based approaches to mental health professionals. Dr. Bertolino is licensed as a marital and family therapist, professional counselor, and clinical social worker in the state of Missouri.

Kevin Thompson, MEd, is Supervisor of the Family Respite Program and a Community-Based Mental Health Professional with seriously emotionally disturbed youth and their families at the Crider Center for Mental Health in Wentzville, Missouri. Previously, he worked in residential treatment as both a direct care worker and as a therapist at several facilities in the Saint Louis metropolitan area. Mr. Thompson teaches workshops on residential treatment, juvenile sex offenders, and collaborative, competency-based approaches to working with youth. He is a member of the American Counseling Association, the International Association of Marriage and Family Counselors, and Chi Sigma Iota, a professional and academic counseling honor society.

CONTENTS

Foreword

The problem is that most people think psychotherapy is something you do. Hundreds of models, theories, and approaches to therapy exist "out there" in which therapists can receive training. They all boil down to a set of actions that therapists do to, or with, the clients who are struggling with aspects of their lives. These models often start from some expert decision or diagnosis about just what exactly is wrong, and this leads to the experts being able to figure out just what needs to be done therapeutically to bring about the desired change. This then usually leads to a treatment plan and/or to some mysterious therapy process that takes place in secret behind closed doors.

This therapeutic work, because it requires expert knowledge and training and can only be undertaken by those who have been initiated into the professional societies, has a certain mystique. As it includes those who are qualified and who have the credentials and affords them a particular status, so it excludes others and affords them an inherently lesser status.

Residential youth care workers have long known their place in the hierarchy. They carry out the day-to-day tasks of caring for young people; organizing them; meeting their physical, emotional, and social needs; teaching them; entertaining them; disciplining them; and so on. When a young person has particular difficulties (or other people experience particular difficulties with a young person), then the experts are called in. The youth care worker prepares the young person for seeing this counselor or therapist, often takes him or her there and waits outside, and helps pick up the pieces afterward. I have sat in on many staff meetings in residential facilities and heard youth workers discuss that a particular young person "needs counseling."

Bob Bertolino and Kevin Thompson have let the secret out! They've trashed the mystique of this thing called therapy and said that anyone can do it—even residential youth care workers.

Are they crazy? It depends on how you think about the therapy process. If therapy remains the activity of experts who can diagnose and treat, then it is crazy to think that anyone can do it. However, Bertolino and Thompson describe the new ideas that have crept into psychotherapy over the past couple of decades. Yet, many professionals still think about the behavioral and emotional problems that adolescents present in terms of pathology and deficit, disorders that must be treated or dysfunctional patterns that must be altered. However, a quiet revolution has taken place as alternate approaches have emerged—approaches that are focused on competency and solution rather than disorder and problem.

These approaches have concentrated on envisioning, encouraging, and building upon strengths and competence rather than fixing or treating deficits or disorders. If therapy is about diagnosing and treating, then it remains the territory of the initiated. If, however, therapy is about identifying and encouraging, then it can be open to a wider range of people. It requires an expert to decide with accuracy "what's wrong" with a young person. Bob and Kevin suggest a different outlook in this book. They suggest that we begin from the question "What's right with youth?" That is a question that anyone can ask, one that begins to lead in a different direction.

This is important. This book is *not* just about a new deal for residential youth care workers. It is not about treating them more as the professionals they are or about recognizing their skills (although it does do both these things). It is not just about entering the territory of other professional disciplines or championing the rights of youth care workers (although it does these things too). No, what is important is that this book starts from a new and different theoretical approach to psychotherapy—and this new approach has implications for who can practice it. It is only because they employ an approach that is based on competency and resources that youth workers can be equal partners in the therapeutic process.

Then, Bob and Kevin go further. They encourage all youth care and therapy professionals to ask different kinds of questions—questions that open up the process to a range of disciplines and allow youth care workers to be actively involved in the real work. They suggest also that these questions open up the process even further. A focus on "what's right" leads us to a focus on change rather than on stuckness and provides a way for youth and family to be part of the process as well.

This is *not* a case of Bob and Kevin saying, "Here's a new expert thing to do. We can tell you what to do—focus on competency and it will work better." Rather, they outline an approach, a different perspective, and the perspective itself leads to collaboration. Collaboration (or "empowerment") is not a new therapy technique. It is the natural consequence of this new focus, of asking different kinds of questions.

Once they've asked this new question, "What's right with youth?," the rest of the book just follows naturally. You'll find yourself thinking, "Yeah, so what's the big deal?" Well, the big deal is that there is no big deal. The big deal is that once we start in a different direction, it all just flows. It all makes sense. In my own professional work, it amazes me sometimes how much of my training has focused on how to make therapy more complicated, more obscure, and, therefore, more professionally exclusive. This book's focus on competency, resilience, and strengths reclaims the common sense in therapy. Once we've done that, there is no big deal.

Bob and Kevin know that residential youth care workers want the best for the youth with whom they work. Why else would they take a job that might include helping with homework, driving youth to various places, making them go to bed, policing household chores, having a "sleep shift" or "overnight," and other activities that are a combination of many roles—parent/teacher/friend/disciplinarian/entertainer/housekeeper? They also show how many traditional approaches lead youth care workers to inadvertently work in ways that bring out the worst rather than the best. However, having begun with that different question, they show how this can start to bring out the best in everybody.

The book's tone is consistent with its subject. It discusses collaboration and that's the way reading it feels. Bob and Kevin don't tell us "how to do it"; rather, they share ideas, they share experiences, and they make some suggestions. (It's just that their ideas, experiences, and suggestions cover just about every aspect of the residential program!)

Bob and Kevin talk about how residential youth care workers are "action oriented." This is true. At the same time, this book is not just about action, about what to do. You see, the problem is that most people think psychotherapy is something you do. This book suggests that therapy is about what you think—or what you *are*. When residential youth care workers begin to think differently, when what they *are* is collaborative and strength focused, then what to do is common sense. This book is great common sense.

Michael Durrant
Department of Psychology
University of Western Sydney Macarthur, Australia;
Author of *Residential Treatment:*
A Cooperative, Competency-Based
Approach to Therapy and Program Design

Preface

Creativity can solve almost any problem. The creative act, the defeat of habit by originality, overcomes everything.

George Lois

Since 1989, Bob has worked at an agency that operates three residential facilities and employs upward of fifty residential youth care workers (RYCWs). Kevin also has spent several years working in a variety of residential facilities. We have both held posts as RYCWs and understand what such positions involve. As do many, we realize that RYCWs are at the very heart and soul of most residential facilities.

In early 1997, through training mental health professionals in competency-based approaches and writing about these ideas (Bertolino, 1999; Bertolino and O'Hanlon, 1998; O'Hanlon and Bertolino, 1998), Bob began to hear some intriguing comments and questions from trainees. These included "I think all of my staff should use these ideas!" and "How can I teach what I've learned to others at my agency?" This echoed what he had thought several years earlier—that therapists weren't the only ones who could benefit from learning competency-based ideas. In the meantime, Kevin and Bob were having ongoing conversations about competency-based approaches, and Kevin was using these ideas on the job as an RYCW. After attending a training program for RYCWs given by Bob, Kevin suggested that this book be written so that other RYCWs could exposed to new ideas and applications.

What we discovered was that many youth-based residential programs have spent significant time and money training staff members, whose responsibility it is is to *do the therapy or treatment*, in collaborative, competency, and strength-based approaches. Even though this shift has been a welcomed one, frontline staff, such as RYCWs—*the ones who spend the most time with youth*—typically have found themselves left out of such training experiences.

We have made it our mission to bring about change in this area. In essence, this book is about filling in this abyss within which RYCWs often find themselves immersed. For those who are "in the trenches" and who work directly with youth on a daily basis, their supervisors and trainers, and the administrators of these programs, this book offers a competency-based perspective that is both clear and practical. In addition, the ideas put forth in this book are both versatile and flexible and can be easily adapted to a variety of settings.

Although a detailed history of the evolution of child care would be outside the scope of the goals of this book, to establish a context for a collaborative, competency-based approach for RYCWs, it's important to understand the journey that has preceded these ideas. Thus, we'd like to begin by briefly exploring the evolution of residential youth care work.

THE EVOLUTION
OF RESIDENTIAL YOUTH CARE WORK

In the Beginning . . .

Prior to 1800, there were only six institutions in the United States catering to children (Tiffin, 1982). Throughout the nineteenth century, almshouses, penitentiaries, juvenile reformatories, and mental and orphan asylums appeared at an accelerating rate. The dominant theme during the nineteenth century was rehabilitation through isolation, obedience, routine, and discipline, along with moral and religious training. Children were often treated the same as adults and cared for along with adults in large congregate institutions. One hundred four institutions for children opened their doors in the nineteenth century (Tiffin, 1982). Patterned after adult prisons, correctional institutions for juveniles began to appear in the 1820s (Levine and Levine, 1970). Cottage care followed in the 1850s, with one cottage mother responsible for managing up to fifty children (Mayer, Richman, and Blacerzak, 1978; Tiffin, 1982)!

In the early twentieth century, a trend evolved from custodial care and rehabilitation toward residential, psychotherapeutic treatment programs. Many states developed standards for licensing programs in the early part of the century, and professionals developed standards for accreditation later in the century. Professionals began to develop procedures for detailed assessment and classification of childhood disorders, and programs began using principles of psychoanalytic theory and learning theory to treat children, with the goal of returning them to the community (Stein, 1995).

Early in the 1900s, Chicago's juvenile court became concerned with the repeated lying, stealing, and sex offenses of children. William Healy was selected to conduct scientific research into the causes of these problems. He established a research project focusing on the causes of delinquency, along with a clinic to treat the behavior problems of children. This clinic was founded in 1909 and was subsequently named the Juvenile Psychopathic Institute because of a prevalent psychiatric opinion at the time that serious antisocial behavior implied serious pathology (Levine and Levine, 1970).

Shortly thereafter, Healy concluded that this opinion was incorrect. He devised detailed and thorough procedures for examination, including obtaining family histories, their social environments, mental and moral developmental functioning, educational backgrounds, friends, interests, occupational efforts, bad habits, and contacts with law enforcement agencies or institutions (Levine and Levine, 1970). A complete medical examination from psychiatric and neurological standpoints and anthropometric and psychological studies was also completed.

During the first thirty years of the twentieth century, government agencies developed programs for visiting and inspecting institutions, while licensing raised standards and increased control. The next twenty years saw the beginnings of the evolution to treatment. In 1935, the Jewish Protectory and Aid Society implemented a new treatment program to create a total therapeutic situation, with increased use of a psychiatrist and social worker. A significant event during this time occurred when Father Flanagan opened Boys Town in Nebraska in 1917.

In the 1930s, many custodial programs became residential treatment centers and new facilities also opened. Based on psychoanalytic theories, the concept of a therapeutic milieu was introduced. Beginning in the 1960s, behavior modification began to appear in residential programs (Adler, 1981). Much was written on token economies and level systems during that time. The trend was that of moving toward smaller, community-based programs.

Current Trends in Residential Youth Care Work

Over the past forty or so years, many new approaches to youth care work have appeared, yet no single theory currently dominates the field of residential treatment. Although behavioral and developmental theories remain the standard, many programs employ a variety of models, principles, and techniques. This is important, given that youth and their needs are unique and require flexible and creative approaches. Despite the flexibility that most programs offer, the predominant orientation toward working with youth typically has remained pathology or problem focused.

Up until the mid- to late 1980s, this also was the case in the field of psychotherapy. However, over the past ten to fifteen years, psychotherapists have experienced an interesting evolution. There has been a shift from pathology- and problem-focused perspectives to more competency-based approaches, such as solution-focused, solution-oriented, narrative, reflexive, possibility, and collaborative language systems therapies (Anderson, 1997; Berg, 1994; de Shazer, 1985, 1988; Eron and Lund, 1996; Freedman and Combs, 1996; Furman and Ahola, 1992; Hoffman, 1993; Miller, Duncan, and Hubble, 1997; O'Hanlon and Weiner-Davis, 1989). This shift also has led to the creation of competency-based approaches specifically for working with children and youth (Bertolino, 1999; Freeman, Epston, and Lobovits, 1997; Selekman, 1993, 1997; Smith and Nylund, 1997). Despite these significant changes, only recently have competency-based ideas begun to surface in working with youth in residential treatment facilities (Booker and Blymer, 1994; Durrant, 1993).

As mentioned earlier, competency-based ideas generally have been filtered through the "main treatment providers" in residential settings, leaving RYCWs out of the picture. This is worrisome because RYCWs generally spend their entire shifts with youth and are in charge of "holding down the fort." They also are the ones responsible for carrying out treatment plans and, ironically, "doing therapy." Not surprisingly, when left only with traditional ideas and blanket techniques (which may not accommodate today's youth),

RYCWs can themselves end up feeling hopeless, with few options. This indeed is a contributing factor in RYCW burnout and high turnover rates. What we will offer is an expansion of ideas for RYCWs that can counter these concerns and engender hope.

WHAT'S DIFFERENT ABOUT THIS BOOK?

The literature for working with youth in residential settings is based primarily on deficit theory and on promoting the "expert" stance of caregivers. That is, there has been, and continues to be, an emphasis on identifying what is wrong with youth, how they are limited emotionally or cognitively, and what they're incapable of attaining or accomplishing. In addition, an expert position has contributed to the idea that mental health professionals, such as RYCWs, know what's best for youth. Although we recognize that, through training and experience, residential care workers certainly do have expertise, so do the youth who are in their respective facilities.

This book offers a perspective that focuses on youth's strengths and competencies, while emphasizing exceptions, solutions, and possibilities. As early as the 1960s, theorists such as Allport (1961) remarked that an emphasis on competency is essential:

> It would be wrong to say the need for competence is the single and sovereign motive of life. It does, however, come as close as any . . . to summing up the whole biologic story of life. We survive through competencies. (p. 214)

Durkin (1990) has stated that an important component in treating illness, particularly in children, involves promoting health, that is, competency. We agree, and add that an overriding twenty-four-hour-a-day, seven-day-a-week concern in residential care should be to promote the normal growth and development of children rather than to focus solely on psychopathology.

Much written work exists regarding the daily routine of RYCWs, the sociodevelopmental needs of the youth in care, and the use of behaviorally oriented techniques for RYCWs. We believe this book supplements and enhances these previous writings, while filling in some formidable gaps in the literature. Our aim is not to suggest a completely new approach, but instead to offer a smorgasbord of competency-based ideas that can serve as an adjunct to what RYCWs are already doing that is respectful and effective.

HOW THIS BOOK IS ARRANGED

In Chapter 1, "A Day in the Life: The Many Faces of Residential Youth Care Workers," an overview of the duties and responsibilities of RYCWs is provided. The notion that RYCWs look at each child as an individual with strengths and competencies and the importance of tapping into these to nurture resilience is explored. It is also proposed that the connection that RYCWs make with youth is the foundation upon which all else is built. For many troubled children, their first positive, long-term, salient, and developmentally significant relationship may be with RYCWs. Finally, the chapter concludes with the assumptions that form the foundation of a competency-based approach.

In Chapter 2 "Something to Believe In: From Impossibility to Possibility," the importance of focusing on what is changeable as opposed to what is not is discussed. To aid movement in this direction, RYCWs are introduced to ways of becoming more competency based in terms of vocabulary. This chapter also includes ideas regarding how RYCWs can use language in a collaborative way to convey respect and facilitate change.

Chapter 3, "Making Contact: Creating a Respectful Context and Climate for Change," begins with how RYCWs can create a context and climate that is conducive to change. The importance of respecting youth and their viewpoints and experiences is emphasized. In addition, ways of using language subtly are offered as a means of opening up pathways with possibilities for change, while simultaneously holding youth responsible for their actions and behaviors. The chapter also involves practical, easy-to-implement ideas about how to conduct competency-based intake assessments and uncover what motivates youth.

In Chapter 4, "We're in This Together: Teaming Up in the Service of Change," the discussion moves to ways that language can be used in treatment planning, staffings, and team meetings. This chapter also includes ideas for working with preestablished level systems.

Chapter 5, "Now You See It, Now You Don't: Altering Problematic Patterns of Viewing," shows how RYCWs can identify problematic patterns in the realms of viewing. Then, specific, practical ways of changing the attentional patterns and stories are offered to help both RYCWs and youth to change unhelpful perspectives. Chapter 5 also includes ways of helping youth to create compelling futures, dissolve barriers, and take action steps toward those preferred futures.

Chapter 6, "Pete and Repeat: Altering Problematic Patterns of Action, Interaction, and Context," focuses on helping RYCWs to identify problematic patterns or the *doing* of problems. Ideas are offered in regard to determining what is not working, what has worked in the past, and what might work in the future.

The next chapter, "'Houston, We Have a Problem': Managing Crisis with an Eye on Possibilities," takes RYCWs into the realm of crisis intervention. Ways of managing crisis, while simultaneously allowing youth to save face, are offered. Also included in this chapter are ways that RYCWs can invite youth into conversations for accountability. Toward this end, the roles of both psychotropic medications and psychiatric labels are explored. Chapter 7 also delves into ideas for on-call workers, and how the lasting impact of RYCWs can make a difference in the lives of youth.

In Chapter 8, "The Journey of 1,000 Miles: Exploring Future Roads with Possibilities," ways of amplifying and solidifying positive change with youth are explored. In addition, ideas for preparing youth for discharge to home or other facilities or situations are discussed. The book concludes with discussions concerning future considerations for RYCWs, including countering burnout and growing to meet the needs of an ever-changing, yet extremely important, field.

Handouts and diagrams are interspersed throughout the book. These materials may be reproduced and used in residential programs.

Bob Bertolino
Kevin Thompson

Acknowledgments

From Bob:

I'd like to thank my wife, Christine, for putting up with me throughout the course of another writing project (and putting up with me in general!). I love you. To my mom and the rest of my family—thank you for your support and for being there—I love you. I'd also like to thank Steffanie O'Hanlon for encouraging me to pursue this book. You recognized the importance of this project, encouraged me to pursue it, and continued to provide support. Thanks to Bill O'Hanlon for being the confidant that you have always been and for reminding me of the multiple meanings of the phrase "learning experience." To Kevin, thanks for friendship and a belief in the good of youth. Last, I'd like to acknowledge the past and present staff of Youth In Need, Inc., in St. Charles, Missouri, with whom I've spent the last nine years. For nearly twenty-five years, YIN has spawned hope for youth and families. Most important are the people who have offered the services and who have shaped the lives of many, including me. I am forever grateful for your contributions to my life.

From Kevin:

I would like to thank Bob for agreeing to do this book with me and for unconditional friendship. I would like to acknowledge the following people who were influential in sparking my interest in the helping professions and in my development as a therapist and as a person: Joel R. Ambelang, Mike W. Jackson, Dr. Z. Maxine Christian, Bill O'Hanlon, and John Denver for his music. I would like to thank my in-laws, Mike and Brigette Smith, for their love, support, and the computer that I used for this book. To Walter Cardona, with whom I've had lengthy discussions about the ideas in this book and whose voice is undoubtedly in these pages—I value our friendship.

Finally, I would like to thank the many colleagues and youth with whom I have had the privilege of working, who have taught me much about themselves, myself, and what is helpful.

From Both of Us:

Thank you to Terry Trepper, Bill Palmer, and the rest of The Haworth Press staff for their tireless efforts and for seeing this book as an important contribution to the field. Thanks also to Rachel Carpenter and Michelle Gorman for comments on the manuscript.

Chapter 1

A Day in the Life: The Many Faces of Residential Youth Care Workers

Life is not so much a matter of holding good cards, but sometimes of playing a poor hand well.

Robert Louis Stevenson

It has long been believed that the "important" therapeutic work in residential facilities is done by the clinical staff composed of psychiatrists, psychologists, counselors, social workers, and so on. This book represents a departure from the traditional view of the residential youth care worker (RYCW) as a secondary facilitator in the process of helping youth to change. We consider RYCWs to be major contributors and factors in helping youth to move on with their lives. Over the next eight chapters, we will offer many different ways that RYCWs can use collaborative, competency-based ideas to facilitate change within residential placements. We'll discuss how RYCWs can become "action oriented."

Before we get started, let's explore "the life and times" of RYCWs, including the types of facilities within which they are employed, their responsibilities, and the commonalities involved with the position.

HERE, THERE, AND EVERYWHERE: PROFILING THE RESIDENTIAL YOUTH CARE WORKER

Youth in out-of-home placements, be they short or long term, are served in a variety of settings, including emergency and runaway shelters, residential treatment facilities, inpatient psychiatric hospitals and units, detention centers, state- and county-operated correctional centers, transitional and independent living programs, group homes, and wilderness treatment programs. Within each of these settings, RYCWs can be found. In fact, although most of the programs mentioned employ some combination of psychiatrists, psychologists, therapists, social workers, case managers, and juvenile officers, by far, RYCWs spend the most time with the children and youth.

Depending on the program, RYCWs are sometimes referred to as resident or youth counselors, psychiatric technicians (techs), child or youth care workers, or house managers. Although the responsibilities and duties of RYCWs may vary from facility to facility and program to program, common factors that run through all of these positions. These include, but are not limited to, the following:

1. Working as part of a team that may include counselors and/or therapists, social workers, case managers, psychologists, psychiatrists, nurses, recreational specialists, and other full- or part-time staff

2. Being responsible for the safety and care of a specified number of youth at any given time (This can vary, but due to licensing requirements, most facilities require a certain ratio of staff to youth at all times, for example, 1:6 or one staff member per six youth.)

3. Being responsible for household or residential duties, such as supervising youth, providing emotional support and discipline, guiding unit or facility meetings and/or groups (e.g., conflict resolution, social skills, psychoeducational, craft oriented, etc.), preparing and taking youth to recreational events (e.g., movies, swimming, sporting events, etc.), assisting with homework, and maintaining the upkeep of the facility and the structure of the program

4. Conducting intake assessments or interviews regarding admittance of youth to the facility

5. Dealing with the variety of crises that can arise with youth or at facilities serving youth

RYCWs carry out a number of daily activities that also can include transporting youth to other facilities and programs, appointments, or meetings. Other responsibilities might involve, but are not limited to, dealing with crisis or emergency hotline calls, writing case notes, distributing medication, and providing elementary first-aid care.

Work schedules for RYCWs can vary greatly. Some will work short, succinct shifts, while others will work twenty-four-hour, thirty-six-hour, or even longer rotations. Schedules can include "sleep shifts," or "overnights," during which a staff member sleeps but is available should a crisis arise. Most facility administrators create schedules and rotations to fit the needs of their programs and satisfy state licensing requirements.

Typically, residential facilities can house anywhere from a handful (such as with emergency shelters when census is very low) to several hundred youth (as with large state-run institutions) (Arieli, 1997). Residential facilities can be very generalized, as with programs that house youth who are in crisis or are homeless, or they can be very specific, such as with inpatient psychiatric facilities and drug rehabilitation programs. In each of these types of placements, RYCWs provide services to youth with a wide variety of backgrounds, situations, and difficulties. In short, RYCWs are immersed in the lives of youth.

THE LONG AND WINDING ROAD: A NEW DIRECTION FOR YOUTH CARE WORKERS

Since their inception, most residential treatment facilities have been guided by parameters based on deficit-based theories. That is, an accepted practice and prevailing view has been that youth or family members are in some way damaged. Michael Durrant (1993) remarked, "Much residential work has reflected ideas of children being damaged or disturbed, children processing some problem or pathology, or parents being incompetent or deficient" (p. 12). According to this perspective, the operational question within many residential programs has been "What's wrong with youth?" The implications of such a perspective on residential treatment are far-reaching. Durrant continues:

> If we approach our task from this viewpoint, inevitably we will see our role as that of experts who operate upon the clients in order to fix or cure something. This view may be reflected in

providing therapeutic care to help children "get over" damaging experiences, exerting control to modify unacceptable behavior and allow control to be internalized, prescribing tasks to alter dysfunctional family structure or processes, and so on. (1993, p. 12)

Because of the deficit/pathology-based paradigm, RYCWs often unknowingly find themselves in a difficult predicament. That is, they become prisoners of systems that succeed in bringing out the worst in youth rather than the best. It is ironic that there are so many needy children and so many good and capable youth care workers, yet the way their relations are structured all too often precludes quality child care (Durkin, 1990).

There are further implications. Due to pathology-based perspectives, many youth who are in residential placements have been subjected to the pessimistic or negative views of others. They have been labeled as "chronic" or "pathological" and as incapable of change. In part because others already have given up on them, these youth often continue to present in the eyes of others as advertised:

Bob encountered a twelve-year-old male, Jeff, who had been placed in the emergency shelter at his agency. At the initial intake assessment, the young man's mother stated, "Jeff's been in two other places and he blew it both times. He just acted like a fool—throwing things and cussing. They said he was headed for jail. They told me I shouldn't let him come home because he's a sociopath and wouldn't change."

Many youth and family members know all too well what it's like to be told that there's little or no hope and that things won't change. They do not need to be subjected to further invalidation. Therefore, we suggest a different question, that is, "What is right with youth?" Such a question leads us in a new direction. It steers us toward competency and change, as opposed to deficit and stuckness.

The Untold Story: Focusing on Competency

Waters and Lawrence (1993) stated that the term *competence* reflects the "belief in people's need to make their world work, to grow and change and to strive for mastery both in the external world and in their internal development" (p. 7). Through our work and our colleagues' work in residential facilities, we have found that promoting competence, rather than emphasizing pathology, can empower youth and facilitate both internal and external change. It also can promote collaborative partnerships between RYCWs and youth rather than adversarial relationships.

A focus on competency means that a belief in change is necessary. Such a position does not mean that we downplay organic or physical propensities and go around chanting affirmations. We do not trivialize or ignore the harsh realities and limitations that youth and those associated with youth experience. Instead, we acknowledge such realities, while simultaneously holding that, although there may be obstacles and roadblocks to negotiate, youth change every day. For RYCWs, the first step in facilitating change is believing in it. Let's return to the case discussed a few moments ago:

> Jeff remained in the emergency shelter program for two weeks. Following his stay, he returned home and attended a couple of aftercare therapy sessions with the therapist who had been assigned to him and his mother. About two years later, Jeff again surfaced at Bob's agency. This time his mother brought him to therapy because of a death in the family for which she thought he had not "grieved." When asked how things had been over the past few years, she remarked, "I don't think it's been any different than with most families. I don't know what the big fuss was before."

Although this particular youth was labeled as a "sociopath" by other mental health professionals, some of which were RYCWs, he did not live out his life by this story. Instead he co-authored a new life story that was facilitated by his family, friends, and the staff members at the third and final facility at which he stayed. This case is not an anomaly. In fact, change of this sort happens every day. We refer to this as the "resiliency factor."

THE HEART OF THE MATTER:
THE RESILIENCY FACTOR

In September 1996, CBS television began broadcasting a series titled *The Class of 2000*, which follows the lives of youth who are attempting to deal with very difficult situations. These youth, despite facing a myriad of unspeakable difficulties, are finding ways of transcending them. One might say that these youth typify the importance of resilience.

According to Michael Rutter (1987), resilience is "the positive role of individual differences in people's responses to stress and adversity" (p. 316). For youth, this relates to situations in which they have lived or grown up in aversive conditions (e.g., poverty, underprivileged circumstances, alcohol/drug abuse, high crime areas, physically/sexually/emotionally abusive environments) and, amid all that has gone wrong or is wrong, have managed to survive (Herman, 1992; Higgins, 1994; Wolin and Wolin, 1993).

Since many youth in residential placements come from difficult backgrounds, they can have significant emotional, biological, neurological, cultural, social, psychological, interpersonal, and physical obstacles to overcome. However, when RYCWs, who are at the core of residential facilities, believe that change is possible and begin to pay attention to what makes a difference for youth, possibilities and opportunities for positive change can be created. Throughout this book, the notion that each youth is an exception and has his or her own qualities of resilience will be emphasized. The same holds true for family members and others involved with youth. Milton Erickson (quoted in Zeig, 1980, p. 220) said, "And so far as I've found in fifty years, every person is a unique individual. I always meet every person as an individual, emphasizing his or her own individual qualities." Although coming from varying circumstances and backgrounds, ultimately, it is attention to the uniqueness of youth and the exceptions in their lives that can make a difference.

MAKING THE CONNECTION:
THE POWER OF RELATIONSHIPS

In 1995, Bob was answering the hotline at the emergency shelter at his work when he received a strange call. He answered, "Youth

In Need, this is Bob; can I help you?" The voice on the other end replied, "You already have." Confused, Bob inquired as to what the person was referring to, as he had no idea. The young man on the other end continued, "Don't you remember me? I was at YIN in 1990 and you helped me." Since Bob had seen hundreds of youth go through the facility, he was having trouble with the question. Soon the young man prompted, "It's Kyle! Remember me?" With the mention of his name, Bob did remember him, and many memories followed. The two talked for a while, and as the conversation neared its end, Kyle lowered his voice and said, "You know, I remember when my dad refused to let me come home and you talked with me. I just wanted to thank you."

To this day, Bob remembers other interactions with Kyle, but not the one Kyle mentioned during that midsummer afternoon phone conversation. In fact, Bob had no idea that one particular interaction would make such a difference. However, what did become clear to him was the difference that RYCWs can make in the lives of youth.

It makes sense that because RYCWs spend more time with youth than other mental health professionals do that they have a variety of ideas with which to work. But, perhaps the most underrated tool that RYCWs bring to the table is themselves. When I (B. B.) talk with youth who are residents in facilities, I frequently hear stories about how a particular staff member made a difference in some way for them. These youth often do not have families, friends, or significant others in their lives that listen or talk with them. Thus, the attention of a caring, empathic RYCW can mean the world to them. In other instances, youth come from intact families or do have others that care, but it's an RYCW who aligns with them and helps to facilitate the change process.

THE TOOLBOX

Many RYCWs have ideas, interventions, and techniques that are *respectful* and *effective* and work very well in their daily work routines. The unique characteristics that each RYCW brings to his or her residential setting are important in facilitating change. It is important to hold on to these ideas!

The assumptions of this collaborative, competency-based approach are meant to build on the existing knowledge and experience that RYCWs possess. It's designed to supplement what RYCWs are already doing that's respectful and effective. Abraham Maslow once said, "If the only tool you have is a hammer, you'll treat the whole world like a nail." This approach, if you will, offers another set of tools that RYCWs can use to better meet the needs of the profession. In the next section, we'll offer a set of assumptions that builds on what each RYCW brings to his or her position.

BUILDING A FOUNDATION: ASSUMPTIONS OF A COLLABORATIVE, COMPETENCY-BASED APPROACH

The following assumptions form the foundation for a collaborative, competency-based approach. Each of the assumptions will be expanded upon over the course of the next seven chapters.

Assumption #1: Youth Have the Resources, Strengths, and Abilities to Change, to Resolve Complaints

The RYCW works to elicit, evoke, and highlight these aspects as opposed to focusing on pathology and deficits. Part of the RYCW's role is to draw out those aspects which youth possess that can help them to overcome obstacles, resolve conflicts, and move on. In the evocation of abilities, strengths, and resources, the RYCW does not try to convince youth or others of anything. He or she merely highlights those virtues, allowing youth and others to establish their own new meanings given new or previously unnoticed information. In a competency-based approach, the main interventive tool in the elicitation and evocation of youth's capacities is language.

Assumption #2: The RYCW Acknowledges, Validates, and Values Youth and Others Involved in All Aspects of the Placement and Therapeutic Process, While Promoting Accountability

Youth need to feel acknowledged and understood. Their feelings, thoughts, and experiences are part of their subjective reality and who they are. All internal experiences are okay; not all actions are okay (e.g., stealing, hurting self or others, etc.). This means that youth can feel what they feel, experience what they experience, and remain accountable for their actions and behaviors (Bertolino, 1999, 1998a; O'Hanlon, 1996a; O'Hanlon and Bertolino, 1998).

Assumption #3: Consideration Is Given to How Aspects or Ideas of Differing Theoretical Perspectives Can Be Unified to Benefit Youth

RYCWs place emphasis on using "what works" with youth. This involves using prior experiences, education, and training to find ideas that complement one another and provide the best possible fit, given the uniqueness of each case. RYCWs find what works and avoid "negatively hallucinating" (when you don't see something that is present) or casting aside ideas to which their theories are "allergic" (Bertolino, 1999).

Assumption #4: RYCWs Maintain a Belief in, and a Focus on, Change

As mentioned earlier, a common misperception of youth today is that they do not have the ability to, or are incapable of, change. This is invalidating to youth and an unhelpful assumption for RYCWs. It is imperative that frontline staff believe that change is possible.

An RYCW who maintains the view that change is possible can convey this belief through the use of language and through interaction. This, in turn, can contribute to the cocreation of new, less oppressive narratives. Conversely, RYCWs who are guided by pathology or unhelpful assumptions that eliminate possibilities for change can create or reinforce narratives in which little or nothing seems possible.

Assumption #5: Direct Care Work Is a Collaborative Endeavor

Duncan, Hubble, and Miller (1997) stated, "Impossibility, we decided, is at least partly a function of leaving clients out of the process, of not listening or of dismissing the importance of their perspective" (p. 30). Working with youth is a collaborative venture. Throughout the entire process of placement, youth are consulted about goals, directions, and the methods being used. This also means collaborating with other family members, professionals, and outside persons who are involved with a particular youth.

Assumption #6: Multiple Realities, Stories, and Truths Are Respected

Parry and Doan (1994) note that no one claim to truth is respected, and "no single story sums up the meaning of life" (p. 10). There is no one *correct* way to view the world, since there are as many realities as people on earth. Craig Smith (1997) remarked:

> No one can form a complete, panoramic, exhaustive view of reality or of the problems clients bring to therapy. Each person involved in the problem scenario would be seen as having a valid yet partial perceptual claim or explanation for what the problem is and what should be done about it. (p. 29)

Youth have particular views which are not always honored but which ought to be. Conversely, although it is important to be sensitive to the different ways that youth view the world, it is also important to attend to those which may be harmful or dangerous to self and/or others. In instances in which such risk exists, RYCWs must take appropriate action to avoid harmful consequences (Bertolino, 1999, 1998a).

Assumption #7: The RYCW, Each Member of the Treatment Team, and the Youth's Broader System Are Cocreators of the Reality Within the Context of Residential Placement Care

There is a physical reality, but subjective reality is observer defined. The worldviews of youth are primarily influenced by biology and personal experiences (e.g., social interactions). The same holds true for RYCWs, who also must contend with theoretical maps and constructions that can greatly alter how they work with and approach youth (Efran and Lukens, 1985).

Residential treatment takes place in the domain of language and social interaction (Berger and Luckmann, 1966). Interpersonal relationships and interactions with others contribute to identities being formed and reformed. We live in different realities, with different people, at different times, with reality being cocreated between each mental health professional and each member of the client system within the therapeutic milieu.

Assumption #8: The Construction of Meaning and the Taking of Action Are Both Essential Considerations

Not all youth will change simply by gaining new meaning in their lives. Saleeby (1994) commented that after people have established some new meaning, they should be encouraged to "begin to create a vision about what might be and to take some steps to achieve it" (p. 357). This is especially important to consider with youth. Oftentimes, youth will need to take action to obtain the change they desire.

The idea of meaning leading to new action also can be a reciprocal process. That is, new actions may lead to the generation of new meaning. Thus, to solely focus on the domain of meaning or the domain of action necessitates leaving out that which may ultimately assist in the resolution of a complaint. A competency-based approach stands in accordance with Thomas Eron and Joseph Lund (1996) who commented, "Effective therapeutic conversations enter the realms of story *and* frame; address meaning and action; and, by so doing, help to resolve problems" (p. 38).

Assumption #9: The RYCW and Each Member of the Therapeutic System, Including the Youth, Have Expertise

The RYCW stakes no claim to preconstructed knowledge resulting from methods and/or theory (Bobele, Gardner, and Biever, 1995) and is not considered an expert on interpreting youth's experiences. RYCWs have ideas that are based on education and experience; however, it is youth who have expertise in their lives. They know what is going on in their lives, what their concerns are, what hasn't worked, and what feels respectful and disrespectful. It is both respectful and collaborative to allow the expertise of youth to emerge in any context. The RYCW can be taught by youth and others what he or she needs to know by allowing each person's story to evolve.

The RYCW's expertise is in creating a context that is conducive to the change process. This includes establishing a safe atmosphere in which young people's stories can evolve and in helping through conversation and/or action to access new pathways with possibilities. This can involve the use of metaphor, stories, ideas, and thoughts that are *offered*, not imposed, as part of an ongoing RYCW and youth dialogue.

Assumption #10: Emphasis Is on Making the Most of Each Interaction with Youth

Often RYCWs underestimate the impact that a momentary interaction with a youth can have. Emphasis is placed on making the most of each interaction by acknowledging each youth's internal experience, holding each accountable for his or her actions, conveying respect, remaining clear, and searching for openings with possibilities for solution and change.

Assumption #11: Orientation Is Toward the Present and Future

When youth feel understood in the here and now, new possibilities for the future can become more apparent. This does not dismiss the possible significance of past events. If a youth is oriented toward the past, the RYCW should be respectful and follow him or her where he or she feels a need to go. However, the RYCW does not hold the assumption that this is how all youth need to resolve their conflicts. It is believed that most youth, when given the choice, will opt to see their problems dissipate in the present rather than returning to humiliating or unsatisfying views of the past. Thus, no preconceived theory suggests that underlying pathologies must be resolved before a youth can move on.

Assumption #12: Youth Help to Define Desired Change and Goals

Youth (and their families, if applicable) determine what needs to be different in their lives, and, hence, where they want to go. They are experts on their lives and generally know what is best for themselves. There are exceptions to this. An obvious one is the establishment of illegal goals, such as aggression, substance abuse, physical/sexual/emotional abuse, discrimination, committing crimes, and so forth. Another is when unrealistic or unachievable goals are set. In the latter case, the RYCW must work within the system to establish more feasible and attainable goals. When realistic goals are established through a collaborative process, RYCWs then know where to intervene and how to help youth to create possibilities.

Assumption #13: It Is Not Necessary to Know a Great Deal About a Complaint, or Its Cause or Function, to Resolve It

Youth solve problems every day. Ironically, problem resolution rarely has anything to do with the explanations that youth or others have about the causes and reasons for their problems. If it did, they wouldn't need help; they could explain their problems away. A concern for RYCWs is that others may seek to know the cause of a particular youth's problem, but often, that's not such an easy thing to pinpoint. Thus, the focus is on promoting change without having to explain it.

In addition, we are aware that problem resolution without the use of explanations can be rapid *and* lasting. It's not possible for us to *discover what the "real" problems are* with youth. That process is too subjective and biased, given that we have only our own realities and theoretical constructions with which to consult. What we can do is work with youth to determine what has or hasn't worked for them and explore avenues of change that do not involve explaining behaviors.

Assumption #14: Change Takes As Long As It Takes

A common argument is whether residential treatment should be brief or long term. From a competency-based perspective, RYCWs work to maximize the effectiveness of each interaction and meeting, with an eye on helping youth to resolve their concerns as quickly as possible. It is not the length of placement that is most important, but collaborating with youth and others to determine where they want to go, when things are better, and when goals have been met. This, by nature, makes for placement that is generally briefer and consumer based. In situations in which residential placement is the only viable long-term option, emphasis is on youth residing in the least restrictive environment that accommodates their needs.

All of the assumptions discussed serve as a *guide* for RYCWs. It is our belief that these ideas facilitate and enhance the change process. We agree with Durrant (1993), who stated:

The aim of residential treatment is that the young person and his or her family should be able to experience themselves as competent and successful. (p. 28)

We would add that rather than working to explain what is happening with youth, RYCWs can learn from youth what they would like to be different in their lives, creating a place to intervene. Then, RYCWs, along with other staff, can work to evoke and elicit strengths, abilities, and resources, while changing youth's views, actions, and the contexts in which their problems linger. These domains will be discussed next.

EXPERIENCE, VIEWS/STORIES, ACTION, AND CONTEXT

From a competency-based perspective, RYCWs can help to facilitate change in four different domains: *experience, stories, action,* and *context*. Table 1.1 offers an outline of these domains.

Experience relates to that which happens internally with a person. This can include feelings, sensations, automatic fantasies and thoughts,

TABLE 1.1. Realms of Intervention

EXPERIENCE	VIEWS/ STORIES	ACTIONS	CONTEXT
• Feelings	• Points of views	• Action patterns	• Time patterns
• Sense of self	• Attentional patterns	• Interactional patterns	• Spatial patterns
• Bodily sensations	• Interpretations	• Language patterns	• Cultural background and propensities
• Sensory experience	• Explanations	• Nonverbal patterns	• Family/historical background and propensities
• Automatic fantasies and thoughts	• Evaluations		• Biochemical/genetic background and propensities
	• Assumptions		• Gender training and propensities
	• Beliefs		
	• Identity stories		

and anything that contributes to the person's sense of self. Experience is very subjective and personalized. Throughout this book, it will be emphasized that all internal experience is okay.

Views come in two varieties. The first relates to what people orient their attention toward or pay attention to in their own lives or situations or in reference to others' lives or situations. The views that people hold can become troublesome when attention is paid largely or solely to problematic aspects of their lives, while other more helpful or less oppressive aspects go unnoticed.

The second type of view is *stories* (e.g., beliefs, assumptions, explanations, etc.) that are based on people's perceptions, understandings, and constructions of meaning. Stories or narratives are how people describe themselves and others. They are negotiable and subject to continual renegotiation. Stories do not symbolize truth, but instead represent a person's perception of the world, created through experience and interaction. Some stories are supportive and spawn hope. Others are problematic or problem saturated, to the extent that the possibility of change seems almost nonexistent.

Actions are what people actually do. As mentioned, some actions are okay and others are not. That is, actions which help clients to achieve their goals and which are healthy, legal, and ethical are okay. Actions or behaviors which move clients away from their goals or which are unhealthy or harmful, illegal, or unethical are not.

Context involves aspects of the person's history and background, including cultural, genetic and biochemical, familial, gender, and spatial and time patterns. Aspects of context can be helpful or unhelpful. They can be problematic when they contribute to the creation or support of a problem. Conversely, aspects of context can be helpful when they stand in support of a person and his or her situation. Oftentimes, helpful aspects of context are buried and/or unnoticed and have to be evoked and elicited.

Throughout this book, numerous ways of acknowledging the internal experiences of youth, while creating possibilities in the domains of stories, action, and context, will be offered. In the next chapter, we will discuss the importance of focusing on creating change and how RYCWs can begin to use language in a collaborative, competency-based way. In this way, pathways with possibilities for present and future change can be explored.

Chapter 2

Something to Believe In:
From Impossibility to Possibility

"There is no use trying," she said. "One can't believe impossible things." "I dare say you haven't had much practice," said the Queen. "When I was your age, I always did it for half-an-hour a day. Why sometimes I've believed as many as six impossible things before breakfast."

Lewis Carroll

A collaborative, competency-based perspective not only hinges on the belief that change is possible but that RYCWs can play a major role in facilitating the change process. We know that change is constant, yet, as previously discussed, RYCWs often find themselves in a position of focusing on how youth remain stuck. In this chapter, we'll introduce ways that RYCWs can begin to shift their thinking and tap into the realm of change with youth. To get us started, let's take a look at Walt Disney, who had some ideas about how to create possibilities and change.

WHAT WALT DISNEY KNEW:
CREATING POSSIBILITIES

Walt Disney had a particular way of envisioning life. Whether making cartoons or feature films, developing new artistic or musical mediums, or building theme parks, he was in a constant state of exploring what was possible. Disney figured that if you can dream something, you can make it a reality:

> When Disneyland was being constructed, Walt would often take park engineers to the site to discuss his ideas with them. During these meetings, it was common for him to convey what he had planned for a certain attraction or aspect of the park, which was sometimes outlandish, and for one or more of the engineers to say, "Walt, we can't do that. It won't work." But Walt was persistent. He had a clear vision of how he thought Disneyland ought to be. So he would ask his engineers to kneel down, view a certain aspect of the park, and tell him what they saw. Why? Because he felt it was the best way to get the engineers to experience the perspective of the children who would be coming to the park. Once the engineers understood the importance of the vision, they would figure out how to make what was seemingly impossible possible. Time after time Disney and his engineers would turn visions into reality. (Thomas, 1994)

What can we learn from this? There are at least two things. First, although we are not creating theme parks here, when we hold the belief that change can happen with youth in residential placements, the seemingly impossible can become possible (Bertolino, 1999). Just as Disney focused on what was possible, as RYCWs, we can orient toward the possibilities of change and convey that to the youth with whom we are working. Again, this does not mean being a "Pollyanna" and downplaying the problems that youth experience. We are not suggesting that if youth "wish upon a star," say enough affirmations, or think positive, everything will be just fine and all their problems will evaporate into thin air. Youth and others associated with youth experience very difficult and debilitating problems. What we are suggesting is that we can acknowledge and attend to youth's circumstances, difficulties, and problems without closing down the possibilities for change.

The second thing that we can learn from Walt Disney stems from the first. To translate his ideas and communicate in a common language with the Disneyland engineers, Walt learned how to read architectural plans (Thomas, 1994). He learned to speak a different language—one that opened up possibilities instead of closing them down. For RYCWs, this translates to a new way of speaking and interacting with youth and others—a shift from a pathology to a competency focus. Let's see how this works.

FROM PATHOLOGY TO COMPETENCY: A NEW LANGUAGE OF CHANGE

As RYCWs and mental health professionals in general, we typically are trained to be "pathology detectors." As discussed in Chapter 1, we are taught to discover, uncover, and explain what is wrong with youth. We come to describe our "discoveries" through language by talking about liabilities, inabilities, deficits, and weaknesses. The difficulty with such language is that it can stigmatize youth, inhibit positive change, and create unnecessary and unhelpful ways of communicating among professionals. So, although we acknowledge the limitations that youth face, we believe that a pathology-only focus closes down possibilities.

We advocate for a "new language of change" (Friedman, 1993). Such a focus helps RYCWs and others to notice what is "right" with youth as opposed to what is wrong. It also invites RYCWs to more fully appreciate human agency and potential (Hoyt, 1994). This transition requires RYCWs to trade in those vocabularies which are unhelpful, disrespectful, jargon filled and which disallow the possibilities for change.

To illustrate this shift in language, we've included some examples of how RYCWs can move from a language of pathology to one of competency (see Table 2.1). The adoption of a new vocabulary and the overall use of this language allows RYCWs to undertake a collaborative pilgrimage to explore the abilities, strengths, and resources that youth and others who are associated with youth possess.

A competency-based vocabulary can empower both RYCWs and youth. It can bring to light that which has previously gone unnoticed, as it requires RYCWs to reexamine and question what they believe about youth. Again, we are not suggesting that RYCWs become positive and Pollyannaish. We acknowledge that youth face limitations in many forms. What we want to do is pay attention to how our

TABLE 2.1. Pathology- versus Competency-Based Vocabulary

Pathology-based	Competency-based
Fix	Empower
Weakness	Strength
Limitation	Possibility
Pathology	Health
Problem	Solution
Closed	Open
Shrink	Expand
Control	Nurture
Fear	Hope
Cure	Growth
Stuck	Change
Missing	Latent
Past	Future
End	Beginning
Judge	Respect
Never	Not yet
Limit	Expand
Defect	Asset

use of language can open up or close down possibilities. To further illustrate this shift, take a moment to answer the following questions:

- Is it important to you to have hope in your life?
- Do you want others to respect you as a person?
- Do you prefer for people to only point out your defects and flaws, or would you also like people to highlight your assets?
- Do you want others to understand you solely on what you've done in the past, or would you like them to know what you aspire to be?
- When speaking about or to you, do you want others to identify what you're incapable or capable of doing in the future?
- Do you want to be in a position of trying to fix youth or to empower them to make their own changes?

What did you find out about yourself? Did you learn something about what you believe? Now, take a moment to ask yourself, "How does what I believe translate to working with youth?"

We believe that it is important to ask ourselves questions such as the previous ones because our beliefs directly impact the way we work with youth. Yet, we must also take this a step further because in our experience, RYCWs who are most effective continually ask themselves, "What's right with this youth (or situation involving a youth)?" These RYCWs are able to establish warm and meaningful relationships with youth and others by conveying respect and hope. To do this, they use language in a way that creates a context and climate for change. In fact, these mental health professionals use competency-based language as a vehicle in a variety of conversations.

We would like to further illustrate the differences between traditional, pathology-based conversations and collaborative, competency-based conversations for RYCWs. To do so, we have included tables outlining each. Table 2.2 shows the ways that RYCWs have traditionally used conversation from a pathology-based perspective. In contrast, Table 2.3 offers ways in which RYCWs can use collab-

TABLE 2.2. Traditional Conversations with Youth

• **Conversations for explanations**
Searching for evidence of functions for problems
Searching for or encouraging searches for causes and giving or supporting messages about determinism (biological/developmental/psychological)
Focusing or allowing a focus on history as the most relevant part of the youth's life
Engaging in conversations for determining diagnosis, categorization, and characterization
Supporting or encouraging conversations for identifying pathology
• **Conversations for inability**
• **Conversations for insight/understanding**
• **Conversations for expressions of emotion**
Eliciting youth's expressions of feelings and focusing on feelings
• **Conversations for blame and recrimination**
Attributions of bad/evil personality or bad/evil intentions
• **Adversarial conversations**
Believing that youth have hidden agendas that keep them from cooperating with treatment goals/methods
Using trickery/deceit to get youth to change
Believing the therapist is the expert and youth are nonexperts

Source: Adapted and modified from the work of Bill O'Hanlon. Copyright © 1996 by Bill O'Hanlon.

TABLE 2.3. Collaborative Conversations with Youth

- **Conversations for change/difference**
  Highlighting changes that have occurred in youth's problem situations
  Presuming change will and is happening
  Searching for descriptions of differences in the problem situation
  Introducing new distinctions or highlighting distinctions with youth

- **Conversations for competence/abilities**
  Presuming youth competence/ability
  Searching for contexts of competence away from the problem situation
  Eliciting descriptions of exceptions to the problem or times when youth
    dealt with the problem situation in a way they liked
  Eliciting and evoking areas of expertise with youth and others

- **Conversations for possibilities**
  Focusing the conversation on the possibilities of the future/goals/visions
  Introducing new possibilities for doing/viewing into the problem situation

- **Conversations for goals/results**
  Focusing on how youth/family members/other mental health profession-
    als, and so on, will know that they've achieved their therapeutic goals

- **Conversations for accountability/personal agency**
  Holding youth/others accountable for their actions
  Presuming actions derive from youth's intentions/selves

- **Conversations for actions/descriptions**
  Channeling the conversation about the problem situation into action des-
    criptions
  Changing characterizational/theoretical talk into descriptive words
  Focusing on actions youth/others can take that make a difference in the
    problem situation

Source: Adapted and modified from the work of Bill O'Hanlon. Copyright © 1996
by Bill O'Hanlon.

orative, competency-based conversations to explore the possibilities of change with youth.

To get a clear view of how the differences between a traditional,
pathology-based conversation and competency-based conversation
might appear in a residential treatment setting, let's explore each
perspective, one at a time. First, here's a dialogue between a RYCW
and a youth that arises from a traditional perspective:

RYCW: Welcome to Midwestern Youth Services.

Youth: Thanks.

RYCW: Where did you come from?

Youth: I was at the Shelton Center.

RYCW: Oh yeah, I know that place.

Youth: I didn't like it there.

RYCW: What didn't you like about it?

Youth: Everything.

RYCW: [Looking at the youth's file] Well, I see that you came here because you were fighting there. What was that all about?

Youth: I said I didn't like it there. The people were mean.

RYCW: Did you try to get kicked out?

Youth: No.

RYCW: What happened then?

RYCW: I don't know.

Youth: I can see that you're on Ritalin, imipramine, and Clonidine for ADHD [attention deficit hyperactivity disorder]. Were you taking your medications?

Youth: Yeah, but it didn't help. It just made me sleepy.

RYCW: We'll fix that when you see your new psychiatrist. Okay?

Youth: I guess.

RYCW: All right. Well, I don't know what it was like at the Shelton Center, but I've got to make sure that you learn the rules here. Okay?

Youth: Whatever.

RYCW: Look, there are rules everywhere.

Youth: I know. It's just like when I was living at home, but worse.

RYCW: I saw that in your file—that you had trouble at home too.

Youth: It wasn't much. My mom didn't want me there after her new boyfriend moved in.

RYCW: I see you've been in four other placements, and in two of them, you got in trouble for arguing with staff and having a bad attitude. Do you understand what you did wrong in those places?

Youth: Nobody would listen to me there.

RYCW: We'll listen to you here, so don't worry about that. But we've still got rules, and you can't do that stuff here. You'll have problems if you do. So here's a list of the rules.

Now, let's explore what this interaction could be when more competency-based conversations are utilized:

RYCW: Welcome to Midwestern Youth Services.

Youth: Thanks.

RYCW: Where'd you come from?

Youth: The Shelton Center.

RYCW: Oh yeah? How'd it go for you there?

Youth: I didn't like it. People were mean there. I got kicked out.

RYCW: I'm sorry to hear that. How long were you there?

Youth: A year and a half.

RYCW: How did you manage to make it there for so long? What did you do?

Youth: I don't know.

RYCW: I was just curious because you must have done some things that helped you to stay there for a whole year and a half.

Youth: I guess.

RYCW: That's fine; you may have some ideas later about what was helpful to you there. I saw in your file that you've been a few different places. You probably know a lot about residential placements, so maybe when you're up to it, you can tell me about what worked for you in some of those places.

Youth: Maybe.

RYCW: Well, my sense about you is that you can do well here. Is there anything we can do right now to help you feel more comfortable and help you to settle in here?

Youth: I don't know.

RYCW: That's fine. Now, we don't expect you to remember all the rules right away, but I want to give you a list so you can at least look them over. You know, I'll bet that you're somewhat of an expert on rules because you've had them everywhere you've been. But if you have any questions about the ones here, just let me or any of the other staff members know. We'll be glad to talk with you about them.

Youth: Okay.

To some, the differences between the two conversations may seem subtle. However, they are distinctly different. First, the traditional conversation focused on some of the following assumptions:

1. Past behavior will indicate future behavior—"I saw that in your file—that you had trouble at home too."
2. There must be a way to explain behavior—"Were you taking your medications?"
3. Insight and/or understanding are necessary—"Do you understand what you did wrong in those places?"
4. Bad intentions may be the cause—"So did you try to get kicked out?"

The collaborative, competency-based conversation also operated from some assumptions. Some of them were the following:

1. Focus on possibilities—"Well, my sense about you is that you can do well here."
2. Assume the presence of competence/abilities—"I was just curious because you must have done some things that helped you to stay there for a whole year and a half."

3. Search for actions/descriptions—"How did you manage to make it there so long? What did you do?"

4. Assume youth have expertise—"You probably know a lot about residential placements, so maybe when you're up to it, you can tell me about what worked for you in some of those places."

Why is it so crucial that RYCWs use collaborative, competency-based conversations as opposed to those which focus on pathology? There are several reasons. First, it is not enough to believe in change; we also must convey that belief through our language with youth. As outlined in Table 2.3, we can do this through a variety of conversations.

Next, we cannot objectively know the *answers* to what a youth has experienced, will experience, or his or her "problems." That is, unless a biological, organic propensity is operating, we can only speculate about the nature of a youth's difficulties. However, some mental health professionals are experts at using pathology-laced language to turn speculation into *unfounded fact*. Problems can be, and often are, *created* through language (Berger and Luckmann, 1966). Our aim is much different. We want to create possibilities within language and promote change. This is precisely why we strive to use conversations that spawn hope and change. We convey the message that we believe that change is *possible* and that it can happen even in the most difficult situations.

Last, when we use collaborative, competency-based language, we have more options and freedom to be creative. For example, how many options can you think of for working with a youth who has been labeled as hyperactive or argumentative or manipulative? On the other hand, how many options can you think of for working with a youth who has a lot of energy, or openly expresses himself or herself or is a creative thinker? The way that RYCWs (and all mental health professionals) use language will either close down possibilities, as with "problem talk," or open them up through "solution talk" (Furman and Ahola, 1992). Table 2.4 offers some further examples of solution talk with youth.

By changing our language and moving from problem to solution talk, we are not minimizing the severity of a youth's problems.

TABLE 2.4. Problem Talk and Solution Talk

Problem Talk	Solution Talk
Hyperactivity	Very energetic at times
Attention deficit disorder	Short attention span sometimes
Anger problem	Gets upset sometimes
Depressed	Sad
Oppositional	Argues a point often
Rebellious	Developing his/her own way
Codependent	People are important to him/her
Disruptive	Often forgets the rules in class
Family problems	Worries about his/her home life
Shy	Takes a little time to know people
Negative peer pressure	People try to influence him/her
Feelings of rejection	People forget to notice/him her
Isolating	Likes being by himself/herself

Linda Metcalf (1995) stated that people "often feel more *heard* when their problem is redescribed, and relax at the suggestion that things are not as bad as they thought. Describing a problem as terrible and difficult rarely motivates people to change" (p. 39). Clearly, how we talk has a direct impact on how we approach problems, solutions, and possibilities. Our suggestion is that, as RYCWs, we use language in a way that supports, validates, acknowledges, and opens up possibilities for change while simultaneously holding youth accountable for their actions. We see this as a necessary process regardless of whether a youth is being seen in outpatient therapy, in a group context, in residential treatment, or in other settings.

WHEREVER YOU ARE, THAT'S OKAY

As discussed earlier, when youth are placed in residential settings, they often get the sense that they are bad, defective, damaged, or, in general terms, "no good." Sometimes this message has been directly given to a youth. For example, a parent might have said, "You'll never change. You're just bad news." It's also possible that a mental health professional, such as an RYCW, might have said, "You're out of control." At other times, a youth may have indirectly come to the conclusion that he or she is bad simply because he or she was brought to therapy or put in a residential facility.

We don't hold the story or idea that youth are damaged in some way or are unable to be helped. Instead, we work in small ways to open up pathways with possibilities for change. In the upcoming chapters, we'll discuss a variety of ways to do this through the realms of views/stories, actions, and context. However, from a collaborative, competency-based approach, our first move is always to acknowledge what youth and others experience internally.

As outlined at the end of Chapter 1, *experience* includes feelings, sense of self, bodily sensations, sensory experience, and automatic fantasies and thoughts. It is impossible to tell another person what to feel or experience. Nevertheless, this occurs with regularity. When this happens with youth, they sometimes get the sense that they're bad simply because of what they are experiencing or will experience. Additionally, it can be further invalidating to youth if they're told, "You shouldn't feel that way" or "Get over it" or "It wasn't that bad." We want youth to have the sense that whatever they experience internally is okay.

We do not consider ourselves to be experts on what youth experience internally. That's the type of expertise that youth bring to a residential setting. What we do is acknowledge and validate all "felt" experience that youth may have and simultaneously work to promote change within other realms. So, although we say that all internal experience is okay, not all actions are.

We have a simple way of thinking about this. First, we stand in support of actions that youth and others undertake that are legal and ethical, that involve healthy choices, and that move them toward their goals. Conversely, we stand opposed to and work to change actions that are illegal and unethical, that involve unhealthy choices, and that move youth and others away from their goals. The distinction is that youth can feel what they feel, think what they think, and experience what they experience, while remaining accountable for what they do.

KEEPING THE LINES MOVING
AND SIGNPOSTS OF CHANGE

For many youth, residential placement can be a long-term affair. This is not necessarily due to the nature or severity of a youth's problems. It is in part due to the large number of youth in state custody, with few placement options available to social services workers in charge of finding homes for such youth. Truly, it can be difficult for youth to find hope when there seems to be little chance that they will know any other life outside of residential placements until "adult" life (which is generally considered to be eighteen years of age in the United States).

Despite the parameters set forth by outside forces, there is always hope. Even in the most difficult situations, it is important that RYCWs make the most of each opportunity they have to promote hope. To do this, once again we call on Walt Disney.

If you've ever been to Disneyland, Disney World, or Universal Studios, it's likely that you experienced an interesting phenomenon and don't even know it. Although the lines are long and it may take an hour or even two to get on a ride, these lines seem to keep moving (Bertolino, 1999; Efran and Lukens, 1985). Rarely do you stand still for very long. In addition, on many of the rides, the entertainment begins once you get in line—televisions with videos playing or sights to see along the way.

What's the point? Although the line would be just as long if you were standing still, people get the sense that they are making progress toward their end goal of getting on the ride. The people at Disney (and now other theme parks too) found that if people feel that they are moving forward, they become less irritated, frustrated, and upset. Let's think about this another way.

On long car trips, you can become overwhelmed knowing that you have far to go to reach your destination. However, if you begin to break the trip down into smaller increments and watch for landmarks along the way, the trip can seem much easier to withstand. For example, if a trip is 1,000 miles, knowing that the Grand Canyon is just an hour away or that the next major city is 120 miles away can make the end goal seem more attainable.

We believe that these ideas are helpful for RYCWs working with youth in residential placements. Many youth will become frustrated and get the sense that they are not making progress toward their end goals. They will lose faith and any sense of hope that their lives can be different. Yet, by identifying "signposts" of change, RYCWs can generate and restore hope in youth by helping them to see that they are making progress. That is, RUCWs can help youth to recognize those small changes that indicate movement toward a larger goal or end point. This, in turn, can give youth the sense that they are growing, maturing, and making progress—that change is happening. This can diffuse some of the frustration and anxiety that youth may experience when there appears to be no light at the end of the tunnel.

We want to be clear that such a process does mean that we try to convince youth that change is occurring. We do not ask youth to buy into our perspectives. Rather, youth convince and teach us that they are changing and making progress through their actions and interactions. In upcoming chapters, we'll investigate ways that RYCWs can help youth on an everyday basis to recognize signs that they are making progress, thus promoting hope.

In the next chapter, we'll begin to put to work the ideas that we've discussed up to this point. We'll explore how RYCWs can use language in the beginning phases of contact with youth and families in residential treatment.

Chapter 3

Making Contact:
Creating a Respectful Context
and Climate for Change

The greater the obstacle, the more glory in overcoming it.

Molière

Now that we have introduced a shift in language for RYCWs, let's explore how to put these ideas to work in a variety of contexts. In this chapter, we'll discuss ways that RYCWs can use collaborative, competency-based language and conversations in initial contacts, face-to-face assessments, and hotline/phone assessments.

FIRST IMPRESSIONS

We've already discussed that it is RYCWs who spend the most time with youth in residential facilities. Further, in many such places, it is the RYCW who is involved in the process of placement from the start. This puts the RYCW in the unique position of often being the first contact for youth who are entering placement. It is impossible to overstate the significance of these initial contacts for RYCWs *and* youth. Both will, of course, enter into initial contacts with beliefs and biases, experience some immediate impressions, and create some assumptions about the other. Based on these assumptions, oftentimes, unhelpful generalizations will follow. Let's explore the implications of this from the perspectives of youth and RYCWs.

Youth: "All These Places Are Alike . . ."

Upon entering a residential placement, a youth can go through any number of internal experiences, emotions, and feelings. We've already talked about all internal experience being okay. However, if a youth experiences his or her initial contact with an RYCW as negative, it can symbolize a repeat of other negative or invalidating experiences at other facilities with other RYCWs or mental health professionals. In other cases, an initial negative experience with RYCWs can further traumatize a youth who has been placed residentially for the first time. That is, he or she might begin to think, "I *am* a problem."

Some youth will anticipate that an RYCW will "lay down the law" or "dish out the rules" before anything else occurs. After all, isn't that an RYCWs job? In other words, youth may enter placements with the expectation that all residential facilities and all RYCWs will be alike. We want to dispel this myth by making any initial contacts positive. We'll discuss more about how to do this in a moment.

RYCWs: "The Forecast Calls For . . ."

RYCWs often are privileged to evaluations, reports, and psychosocial information before ever meeting youth. Such "rap sheets" can be helpful in gaining an understanding of a youth's history and possibly some patterns in his or her behavior. They also can offer helpful information about a youth's familial and social history. Conversely, we know that prior information can set off sirens within RYCWs and lead to unhelpful assumptions, such as "This kid's got a history a mile long. We're in for trouble" or "He's been diagnosed with ODD [oppositional defiant disorder]. We can expect him to be defiant toward authority" or "She's been in Girls Town so she must be a hard-core case."

What if RYCWs enter their initial contacts with youth with the aforementioned or other similar, preconceived negative views? If a youth initially is well-behaved during the first contact with an RYCW, will his or her history overshadow what the RYCW observes? For example, will an RYCW think, "He's only putting on a front" or "She'll be in a honeymoon phase for a while and then we'll see the 'real' her." Clearly, each of us views situations and the world through different "lenses" that are based on our experiences, both personally and professionally.

In residential treatment, the lenses that RYCWs peer through are especially significant. In fact, the messages that RYCWs send to youth during the first contact can set the tone for how placement begins and, perhaps, what happens over the course of an entire stay (and we would say beyond that too!). Thus, if an RYCW only sees a youth through the lens of previous case histories, a youth may be doomed from the start and unable to escape such negativistic and closed-down views. However, if an RYCW can bring to the initial contact the view that who the youth is as a person supersedes his or her treatment-based paper trail, the positive impact can be limitless:

> Bob was supervising a therapist, Eric, who was working a weekend shift as an RYCW at the emergency shelter. During his shift, a youth named Tom was admitted to the program. Tom was placed due to his father being arrested on drug charges. Eric was one of Tom's initial contacts, and he made an immediate positive impression on the youth. Although Eric knew some of Tom's history (he asked questions out loud then answered them himself, had a history of drug usage, and was described as "strange"), he approached him in a caring and optimistic way.
>
> A few days later, Bob was approached by the Director of Family Development Programs. She stated that the emergency shelter coordinator, Michelle, had come to her because she knew that Eric had made a positive impression on Tom. Michelle had asked if Eric might be able to "check in" with Tom periodically during his stay. Eric did so until the youth was discharged.

Eric could not have known that his initial interaction with Tom would make such a difference. In fact, RYCWs routinely underestimate the impact that they bring not only to initial contacts but *all* interactions with youth. In psychotherapy, research has demonstrated that therapists' attitudes, particularly in the opening moments of therapy, can greatly influence clients' expectations for change (Miller, Duncan, and Hubble, 1997). Therapists who emphasize possibilities and the belief that things can work out can help build hope for clients. Conversely, attitudes of pessimism, an emphasis on psychopathology, or a focus on the long-term nature of change can adversely affect clients.

For RYCWs, the same holds true. In many instances, youth have already directly or indirectly been sent the message that they or their situations are impossible. Holding such an attitude—that youth cannot change—is not only invalidating, it's counterproductive. When RYCWs hold the belief that change is possible, they can begin to convey that to youth during initial and all subsequent interactions.

FACE-TO-FACE ASSESSMENT

Youth are brought to residential facilities by parents, legal guardians, social services workers, juvenile officers, and other law enforcement personnel (i.e., if protective custody is the step that has been taken). Upon arrival, a face-to-face intake assessment is often the starting point. In many facilities, the intake process is merely a formality to gain further psychosocial information. In other placements, the initial face-to-face interview is necessary to determine whether a youth is "appropriate" for admittance. That is, some facilities are locked and some are not. Some will work with extreme behaviors such as aggressiveness; some will not.

An intake assessment or interview can take anywhere from twenty or thirty minutes to several hours, depending on the criteria set forth by the facility. Sometimes youth will be seen with their family members, legal guardians, or others. Sometimes they will be seen individually. Still some programs will have several parts to their initial interviews, requiring that certain people be present at certain times.

Intake assessments can vary greatly but tend to reflect an overall philosophy of a residential facility. Although such interviews are important in the gathering of information regarding a youth and/or family, they need not be a method of pathology detection. In fact, face-to-face assessment can provide an opportunity to facilitate the change process.

In psychotherapy, research has demonstrated that the effects of the client-therapist relationship can contribute as much as 30 percent to outcome (Lambert, 1992). Clients who are engaged and connected with the therapist may benefit the most from therapy. Additionally, a therapist who is empathic, genuine, and respectful contributes to a positive bind or alliance between the therapist and client (Rogers, 1951, 1961). Perhaps most important are clients' perceptions of the therapist as being warm, empathic, trustworthy, and nonjudgmental (Miller, Hubble, and Duncan, 1995; Miller, Duncan, and Hubble, 1997).

Similarly, for RYCWs, it is crucial that a respectful context and climate for change are established during the initial assessment. We have outlined several components of an intake process that we believe can facilitate the process of change:

1. Let youth, family members, social services representatives, juvenile officers, and others tell their stories.
2. Begin to use collaborative, competency-based conversations through questioning.
3. Gain a clear vision of the placement goal.

Let's explore each of these components.

Breathing Room: Letting the Story Unfold

People need to be heard, validated, and acknowledged. Our aim is to ensure that we convey this from the start—during any initial contacts and throughout involvement with a youth and his or her family and significant others. To do this, we begin all contacts by letting the people start wherever they want. Why is this necessary? There are several reasons.

First, when an RYCW starts by asking a series of assessment-based questions without allowing others to relate their stories, it's as if the RYCW is applying a model to the situation regardless of the person or the circumstances. The uniqueness of the situation and the youth becomes obsolete, with a "one model fits all" mind-set taking precedence (Bertolino, 1999). Milton Erickson (Rossi, 1980; Rossi, Ryan, and Sharp, 1983) taught us that we ought to be client driven, not theory driven. Thus, we don't begin with a "cookie cutter" approach. Instead, we ask a more neutral question such as, "Where would you like to start?" or "What should we talk about first?"

A second reason comes from psychotherapy circles. According to Lawson, McElheran, and Slive (1997), "Research indicates that for many clients, the most valuable aspect of the therapy session is the opportunity to tell their story and be heard" (p. 15). For RYCWs, this means that if we attempt to move in a direction prede- termined by an assessment tool, the person may go unheard. If we did this in our everyday conversations, people would walk out on us or stop talking. Thus we begin each assessment by letting the per- son decide where he or she wishes to start. The idea here is that youth and others ought to have space for their stories to be told and heard (Bertolino, 1999).

There is a third reason that the telling of each person's story is crucial. If a person is cut off before having the space to relate his or her perspective, the RYCW risks not learning about the person's understandings of the problem and previous attempts to solve it. Further, it can be disheartening to a youth when RYCWs, in an attempt to resolve a crisis, suggest approaches that have already been unsuccessfully tried. By allowing each story to unfold the RYCW can attend to that which has worked and that which hasn't for the youth and family.

Now, it is not necessary for people to ramble on aimlessly or tell their entire life stories to feel heard. In fact, many RYCWs will be in charge of multiple tasks simultaneously and have to attend to and supervise the youth in their respective facilities. Thus, they cannot be occupied for long periods of time. So as people tell their stories, the RYCW begins to do two things. First, openings can be introduced through collaborative, competency-based language. That is, we can acknowledge and validate each person's experience and inject the element of possibility at the same time. Second, we can help them to gain a focus on what they would like to change. This is crucial because oftentimes people who are in crisis aren't sure what they want.

Painting Doorways in Corners:
Acknowledgment and Possibility

As parents, social service workers, juvenile officers, youth, fami- ly members, legal guardians, and others give information and tell their stories, RYCWs do not have to remain stagnant and try to maintain constant neutrality. Instead, RYCWs can begin to offer pathways with possibilities through language. For this, we refer to Carl Rogers (1951, 1961) who taught us about the importance of empathy and acknowledgment.

Rogers related that from the start, people need to feel heard and understood. If this does not happen, they will likely close down, become angry, or let the RYCW know in some way that there is a problem. This is a crucial aspect that we must attend to from initial contacts and *throughout any placement and therapeutic process.*

Still, as we listen and attend to youth and others, if we only reflect back their experiences, many will continue to box themselves into corners. They will describe situations that seem hopeless, with no way out. All the pure reflection in the world will not change that.

Thus, what we want to do is add a twist to the idea of pure reflection (Bertolino, 1999; O'Hanlon, 1996b; O'Hanlon and Beadle, 1994; O'Hanlon and Bertolino, 1998). Many of the old Warner Brothers cartoons show the Roadrunner character trapped in a corner by Wile E. Coyote. However, just when it seems that Roadrunner is doomed, he seems to find a way out. One of the ways he does this (and he does it time and time again because it works!) is by painting a doorway with a knob on a wall, opening the door, and escaping. Through the use of language we can do the same. We can help people to move out of the corners they have talked themselves into by offering them new possibilities through language. Here are three ways of doing this:

Reflect back youth's and others' responses or problem reports in the past tense. Here are some examples of how to do this:

Parent: He's always in trouble.

RYCW: So he's been in trouble a lot.

Social Services Worker: He keeps running away.

RYCW: He's run away many times.

Youth: I'm bad.

RYCW: You've felt bad about yourself.

During our interactions, when a youth, parent, or other person gives a present-tense statement of a problem, we acknowledge and reflect back the problem using the past tense. This is not pure Carl Rogers because we are moving beyond basic reflection. We are acknowledging and validating people where they are and also moving into the realm of possibilities at the same time.

Take youth's and others' generalities such as everything, everybody, nobody, always, and never and translate them into partial statements. This can be done by using qualifiers related to time (e.g., recently, a while ago, in the past month or so, most of the time, much of the time), intensity (e.g., a bit less, somewhat more), or partiality (e.g., a lot, some, most, many). We do not want to minimize the youth's or other's experiences or invalidate them. Instead, we want to gently introduce the idea of possibilities. The following are some examples:

> **Parent:** He gets in trouble all the time.
>
> **RYCW:** So he gets in trouble a lot of the time.

> **Youth:** Nothing ever goes right for me.
>
> **RYCW:** Sometimes it seems like nothing goes right.

> **Social Services Worker:** He just can't stop.
>
> **RYCW:** Recently, you've been feeling as if he can't stop.

The idea is to go from global statements to partial ones, while continuing to acknowledge and validate the person. We want to create a little opening where change is possible.

Translate youth's and others' statements of truth or reality—the way they explain things for themselves—into perceptual statements or subjective realities. Here are some ways to do this:

> **Parent:** I'm a bad mother because my kid's always in trouble.
>
> **RYCW:** So you've really gotten the idea that you are a bad mother because your kid's been in trouble.

> **Parent:** He'll never amount to anything.
>
> **RYCW:** Because of what he's done, it seems to you that he'll never amount to anything.

Youth: I'm evil.

RYCW: Your sense is that there is evil in you.

Youth's and others' statements about youth are not the way things are, but the way they have perceived or experienced a particular situation. By reflecting back their statements as perceptions, we can introduce the notion of possibility. This process becomes a part of the flow of the phone assessment and helps to establish a context of change through constant acknowledgment and the opening up of possibilities through language.

If the RYCW doesn't validate youth and others, if it sounds like a minimization, or that they are being pushed to move on, the youth or others will react. They will say things such as the following:

Parent: Not most of the time! All the time!

RYCW: Okay. Up to this point, he's been bad all the time.

If the person reacts this way, we are not getting it right. We want to validate them and introduce possibility—*Up to this point, he's been bad all the time.* This validates the perception while putting it in the past tense. These are subtle linguistical shifts, invitations rather than coercion or judgments. Youth have usually heard enough of that type of talk, which generally translates to invalidation and blame for them. So we are not trying to dissuade anyone out of his or her perceptions and experiences. Instead, we want to offer up the idea that even though his or her world has been difficult, change is possible.

By combining acknowledgment and validation with possibility, we can listen to the stories that are brought to assessments (and all conversations thereafter) and simultaneously inject some hope into the situation. Ironically, there are times when this process can help to normalize the experiences of a parent or guardian, who may then decide to try outpatient therapy or another route instead of opting for residential treatment.

When acknowledgment and validation are combined with language of change and possibility in ongoing RYCW reflections, youth can begin to shift their self-perceptions. In addition, those who are associated with the youth can begin to alter their own perceptions of them. Although this process may begin during the assessment phase, ultimately it represents a continuous process throughout residential placement whereby youth or others can come to a more possibility-oriented sense of themselves.

The following is a case example of how one can begin an assessment and interject possibility-laced language. A twelve-year-old named Will was brought in to an emergency residential placement by his mother after stealing the family car and running away. His mother felt that she could not "control" him and sought a family "time-out." This meant having her son placed residentially for a couple of weeks. Here is how the assessment began:

RYCW: Where would you like to begin?

Mother: Everything's such a blur. I mean, I thought everything was fine and then all of the sudden he pulls these stunts.

RYCW: So until recently things were moving along okay— then the things you mentioned happened?

Mother: Yeah. I still don't know where he got the idea of stealing the car. That was just plain dumb! Then there's the runaway thing. I have no idea what's going on, but I don't like it. It's scaring me.

RYCW: So you're not sure where he got the ideas about stealing the car and running away. What's most scary about what you've been experiencing?

Mother: I'm afraid that he's going to end up in more trouble and then he'll be locked away for good.

RYCW: I see. You're worried because he's done some things that have led you to believe that he might be heading for more trouble—and that might include being locked up. Is that right?

Mother: Right.

RYCW: Is that what you're most concerned about?

Mother: Without a doubt.

RYCW: Okay. Is there anything else?

Mother: Well, there's little things, but I just don't want to lose him.

RYCW: I can understand your concern. [Turns to Will] Will, what do you think is happening?

Will: She gets mad at everything.

RYCW: Okay, she's been mad at you sometimes—because of your actions.

Will: I guess.

RYCW: Is that what you're most concerned about—that she sometimes gets mad at you?

Will: Yeah, but she never lets me see my friends.

RYCW: Okay, so another part of it, for you, is maybe that you want to be able to see your friends more often than you have been.

Will: Yeah.

By opening with a neutral question, this mother was able to begin where she wished and tell her story. As she did, the RYCW acknowledged her and simultaneously offered possibilities through subtle changes in language. The same was done with Will. It is important that each person has the sense that he or she is being heard and understood and that his or her problems are not static. These subtle offerings through language can inject the element of possibility into situations that *appear* to be closed down.

Using Collaborative, Competency-Based Conversations Through Questioning

As discussed earlier in this chapter, it is commonplace for mental health settings that serve youth and families to use a universal or agency-designed assessment tool to gather information. Some places will require only that minimal information, such as demographic data and a brief social history, be obtained. Others will require in-depth and lengthy procedures using rather complex assessment tools, often leading to a psychiatric diagnosis for a youth. Table 3.1 offers an example of an intake assessment form.

TABLE 3.1. Sample Intake Assessment Form

INTAKE ASSESSMENT

YOUTH INFORMATION

Name of Youth:_____ Age:_____ Date:_____

Date of Birth:_____ Gender:_____ Race:_____

Address:_____

City:_____ State:_____ Zip Code:_____

Phone Number:_____

PARENT/LEGAL GUARDIAN INFORMATION

Circle One: (N, S, A)   Circle One: (N, S, A)

Mother:_____   Father:_____

Address:_____   Address:_____

Home Phone:_____   Home Phone:_____

Work Phone:_____   Work Phone:_____

Siblings:

Name	Age	N, S, A	Residence
_____	___	___	_____
_____	___	___	_____
_____	___	___	_____
_____	___	___	_____
_____	___	___	_____

Name of Legal Guardian:_____

Address:_____

City:_____ State:_____ Zip Code:_____

Home Phone:_____ Work Phone:_____

REFERRAL SOURCE

Referring Person:_____

Agency Name (if applicable):_____

Address:_____

City:_____ State:_____ Zip Code:_____

Phone Number:_____

Assessment does not translate to simply discovering or uncovering pathology. In recent years, with an emphasis on more collaborative and competency-based approaches, clinicians have created innovative ways of interviewing clients for not just problems, deficits, and limitations but also strengths, abilities, and resources (Berg, 1994; Bertolino, 1999; Durrant, 1993, 1995; O'Hanlon, 1996c;

Education History: (Circle One)
    a. Attending regularly   d. Dropped out
    b. Attending irregularly (extended truancy)
    c. High school diploma/GED
Details:_____
_____
_____
_____

Employment History: (Circle One)
    a. Part-time   d. Not currently employed, not
    b. Full-time   looking for work
    c. Not currently employed, looking for work   e. Never employed
Details:_____
_____
_____
_____

Medical History:
_____
_____
_____
_____
_____

Psychiatric History (including hospitalizations):
_____
_____
_____
_____
_____

Psychiatrist:_____ **Phone Number:**_____
    Current Medications:_____

Psychologist:_____ **Phone Number:**_____
Therapist/Counselor:_____ **Phone Number:**_____

Selekman, 1997). Thus, intake assessments offer an opportunity to both gather information and simultaneously facilitate the change process.

Should a particular residential setting require that a certain type of pathology-based assessment be completed, a respectful and collaborative way is to let the youth and others who are present know

TABLE 3.1 *(continued)*

Placement History:
History of Abuse (specify whether physical, sexual, emotional, neglect, or combination thereof):
Hotline Call Placed: Yes   No   Date:_____
Assessment Summary:
Admission Approved (if no give details)? Yes   No _____
Assessment Completed by:_____
Signature:_____   Date:_____

that everyone goes through the same or similar procedures. This can normalize the process. In these instances, the RYCW can complete the required assessment and then move to a more competency-based focus. Bob (Bertolino, 1999) has written about some ways of introducing youth and families to standard assessment procedures set forth by agencies:

> There are some questions that I need to ask you that we ask of everyone who comes here. First I'll ask you some questions that will tell me about what's going on that's a problem for you. Once we get through those questions we'll move on to some others that will tell me more about what you do well and what works . . . There are two parts to this interview. The first part will involve questions that will give us an idea of how things have become troublesome. The second part will allow us to talk in a different way about your situation. (p. 31)

Some assessments may be pathology or problem focused, but allow room for the RYCW to ask other questions that introduce some sort of balance and that work to elicit and evoke competencies and resources. For example, an RYCW can ask about the problem and then inquire about exceptions or past successes. In these cases, concurrently, information can be garnered about strengths, abilities, and resources in addition to problem areas. Here's an example of how an RYCW might go about this:

RYCW: What school do you go to?

Youth: Abbott Middle School.

RYCW: What grade are you in?

Youth: Seventh.

RYCW: Great. What's school like for you?

Youth: It's stupid.

Parent: He's failing everything—all his classes. That's part of the problem.

Youth: I'm not failing all my classes!

RYCW: Tell me about that.

Youth: I'm passing science and gym. I've got a C in science and a B in gym.

RYCW: Really? [To parent] Is that right?

Parent: Well, yeah. I guess he's passing two of them.

RYCW: [To youth] How do you explain that, although you haven't done too well in some of your classes, you've managed to do better in two of them?

Youth: I don't know.

RYCW: I wonder what you've done differently in the classes that you are passing.

Youth: I just have to go to gym.

RYCW: Sure, but do you have to dress and participate?

Youth: Yeah.

RYCW: I've heard from many youth who won't dress and participate even if it means failing. So I'm curious, how do you get yourself to do that when maybe sometimes you don't want to?

Youth: I just do.

RYCW: Okay. What about science? How have you managed to hold a C?

Youth: Sometimes I do good on tests.

RYCW: Great! How do you do that?

Youth: I just do.

RYCW: Is it because you study or because you listen well in class or something else?

Youth: I guess I just listen better.

RYCW: Okay. Well, I'm wondering about something. I wonder how what you've been doing in gym and science class might be helpful to you in raising your grades in the other classes. You may or may not know the answer, but it might become clear to you later.

Even when the situation seems to be very problematic, the RYCW can consider "What else?" and make use of exception-oriented questions (de Shazer, 1988, 1991; O'Hanlon and Weiner-Davis, 1989; Selekman, 1993). These questions ask for information about when a problem is less dominating, occurs less frequently, is absent, and so on. In turn, the information gathered can form building blocks for future change.

As evidenced by the previous case example, it is helpful, but not necessary, for a youth or others to respond to exception-oriented questions. In fact, many youth will respond with "I don't know" when faced with such questions. The importance of these questions is that they suggest a shift in view and simultaneously imply that there are times when the problem is less oppressive in their lives. This orients youth and others to "what's right" with themselves or their situations. The following are more examples of questions that search for exceptions:

- When does the problem seem less noticeable to you? What is everyone doing when it's less noticeable?
- When does the problem seem to happen less?
- What do you suppose keeps you (him or her) from going off the deep end with trouble?
- What are you (is he or she doing) when you are (he or she is) not in trouble?
- What is it like when the problem is a little less dominating?
- What's it like when things are a bit more manageable? (Bertolino, 1999)

Notice that these questions do not inquire about extremes. We don't ask "When don't you have the problem?" That's too big a leap for most youth, family members, and others. Instead, these questions work to elicit small exceptions. As RYCWs, all we are searching for is a thread of hope or a ray of light. That can be enough to get the ball rolling early on.

By asking exception-oriented questions along with ones that are required on mandated assessment tools, RYCWs can gain valuable information from youth and others who are involved. In addition, hope can be injected into what can often be a very negative experience for youth. If an initial assessment involves focusing only on everything that is or has gone wrong with the youth, it can be further invalidating and a replication of what he or she has already heard on countless occasions. The same can hold true for parents or guardians who may feel as if they have failed, given what they have had to reveal or describe in the assessment.

Each category on an assessment allows many possibilities in regard to exception-oriented questions. The following are examples of exception-oriented questions that can be asked during an initial assessment:

The Problem

- When do you seem to get more of an upper hand with your problems and are not so pushed around by your behavior? How do you do that?
- When things are going poorly, how do you (does he or she) usually start/stop your (his or her) behavior? What do you do to help the situation that's different?
- What have others failed to notice about your situation or problem?

School

- What's something that you can tolerate about school and maybe even enjoy about it sometimes?
- Which of your teachers do you get along with best? (Or, Which of your teachers drives you the least crazy?)
- How have you managed to pass in previous years? (Or, How have you managed to pass [a particular] class?, if the youth failed all but one, for instance)

Placement History

- How have you managed to survive in placement?
- How have you managed to keep your head up when things haven't gone so well?
- What's the longest you've gone in one placement? How did you do that?

Social Relationships

- Who recognizes that you have something else to offer, other than the problem for which you're here?
- Who can you go to when you need help?
- When are your friends most helpful to you?
- What people have you met who have made a positive difference in your life?

Previous Therapy/Counseling Experiences
(Residential or Otherwise)

- What has been helpful about previous experiences in therapy?
- What made a difference for you?
- What wasn't as helpful?

General Questions

- What do other people not know about you?
- What do you want other people to know about you? (Bertolino, 1999)

RYCWs can ask exception-based questions in many areas during the initial assessment. We would add that from this perspective, assessment is not a one-time affair. Although an intake or preliminary assessment may be necessary for entry into a program or facility, in actuality, the process is ongoing. Assessment may begin with an initial interview, but it continues throughout as established goals are met, modified, and changed. Again, youth, families, and their problems are not static.

Gaining a Clear Vision of the Placement Goal

At this point, let's do a brief review. During initial assessments, as RYCWs meet with youth, family members, and others, each person's story is heard and acknowledged as valid. As this happens, RYCWs simultaneously begin to use language to open up the possibilities for change. Once the assessment has progressed to specific form-based questions, the RYCW takes the opportunity also to ask questions that are exception oriented. That is, the RYCW inquires about "What else?" This allows for strengths, abilities, competencies, and resources to be explored within the "problem" context.

The final component of the intake assessment that RYCWs are concerned with is gaining a clear vision of the goal of placement. Typically, two main types of situations involve placement. First, youth are placed because they are homeless, have committed crimes, or have been removed from their homes due to some form of abuse or extenuating circumstances. In these cases, the goal is generally to provide a structured, safe place for the youth to stay and to help them to make the transition to somewhere else (e.g., home, a foster home, another placement, etc.). This often is the situation in which social services or court personnel representatives place youth. In these cases, we want to gain a vision of what will constitute a successful placement in the eyes of the person placing the youth, as well as in the eyes of the youth.

The second type is more often associated with youth who are placed by parents or legal guardians. In these cases, the rationale for placement is sometimes unclear. For example, a parent may feel something is wrong, but not have a clear sense of what specifically is wrong. They may seek a family time-out or break to clear the air. The problem is, if the parent isn't sure what the problem is, then how will he or she know if the placement has been helpful or not? In addition, how will the parent's son or daughter know what is expected of him or her? Thus, the RYCW's task is to work in collaboration with people to clarify what their concerns are. The focus becomes one of creating goals that are both achievable and solvable (Bertolino, 1999). Achievable goals consist of youth's, parents', or others' actions or conditions that can be brought about by their actions.

Action-Based Language and Videotalk

In either type of situation, we want to be clear about the goal of placement. To help people clarify their concerns and for RYCWs to gain a clear picture of the complaint(s), we turn to *action-based language*. By using action-based language, RYCWs can help youth and others to translate vague descriptions and non-sensory-based words and phrases (e.g., "He's a troublemaker," or "She's out of control") into clear, observable, and solvable terms. For example, if a parent claims that his or her son or daughter has a "bad attitude," the RYCW inquires as to how the son or daughter *expresses* a bad attitude. That is, what does he or she *do* that signals the parent that a bad attitude is present?

Below is an example of how an RYCW can use action-based language to obtain a clear description of a complaint:

> **Parent:** My worst fear is that Lisa will continue to act out at school and eventually get suspended or expelled.
>
> **RYCW:** So that I'm clear about your concern, what specifically does Lisa do when she acts out at school?
>
> **Parent:** Well, she gets up and walks around the room and interferes with other students who are trying to do their work.
>
> **RYCW:** Okay. So sometimes she gets up out of her chair and walks around the room. How does she interfere with other students? What does she do?
>
> **Parent:** She hits them on the hands and messes up their writing, or sometimes she waves her hands in front of their faces and tries to distract them.

As an adjunct to action-based language, RYCWs can use *videotalk*. This involves getting youth and others to describe the problem as if it can be seen on videotape (Bertolino, 1999; Hudson and O'Hanlon, 1991; O'Hanlon and Bertolino, 1998; O'Hanlon and Wilk, 1987). Here's one way that RYCWs can use videotalk:

> If you were to videotape your son or daughter being out of control, and I was to watch that tape, what would I see happen-

ing? What specifically would he or she be doing that would indicate to me that he or she was out of control?

By using action-based language and/or videotape descriptions, the RYCW can gain a clear picture of the complaint. Since, oftentimes, youth enter residential placement with psychiatric labels, action language also can be helpful in translating such labels into process or action descriptions. Again, this will help the youth and others, the RYCW, and, ultimately, other team members in the facility to cocreate a solvable problem. Here's an example of how to do this:

Parent: Katie was diagnosed with ODD [oppositional defiant disorder] recently. I mean, what are we supposed to do with her? That just confirmed to us that something is wrong. We have no idea how to deal with her. Our other kids aren't ODD.

RYCW: Okay, I can see how this might be frustrating to you. So that I can be clear about this, I'd like to ask you a couple of questions. Is that okay?

Parent: Sure.

RYCW: Many kids have had the diagnosis of ODD and they've been able to have wonderful lives. What I'm wondering is, what specifically is it that Lisa has done that concerns you the most?

Parent: She fights with other girls in the neighborhood.

RYCW: What kinds of fights?

Parent: Really bad physical ones. I mean, they just pound on each other. She gets really violent.

RYCW: And you're worried probably for a variety of reasons. She might get hurt or hurt someone else . . .

Parent: Yeah, and we don't want her to deal with her conflicts that way.

RYCW: I see. You'd like her to resolve her conflicts without violence. Is that right?

Parent: Exactly.

What we want to do is translate labels into action terms so we can have a clear picture of what the youth is doing that is of concern. As noted in Chapter 2, we have many more options when we are able to take words, labels, or phrases, such as ADD (attention deficit disorder), ODD, depression, out of control, bad attitude, and so on, and turn them into concrete "doable" things. In fact, it's much easier to tackle the complaint of a youth not completing his or her homework than it is to confront the entire concept of ADD.

How Will You Know When It's Better?

Once what needs to change and the goal of placement are clear, it is important for RYCWs to help youth and others to gain a sense of what things will be like when they are better. That is, in the short term, how will people know that a placement has been helpful? Also, in the longer-term scheme of things, what will indicate to them that the situation is better? We again rely on action-based language and videotalk to gain clarification.

Many options are available to RYCWs at this juncture. One possibility is to ask the following questions:

- Let's say that this placement has been helpful in getting things back on track—how will you know?
- What will your son or daughter be doing that will indicate to you that things are better?
- When you feel that your son or daughter has turned the corner and is doing better, what will he or she be doing?

By using action language, clarification can be gained regarding people's expectations in behavioral terms. This is essential for youth because they learn, perhaps for the first time, what is expected of them through specific descriptions. Further, finding out what will determine like when change has occurred is an important process because if people don't have a sense of what better is, they may not recognize improvement. In addition, oftentimes, some small change has taken place prior to the intake assessment that, as RYCWs, we can't know about unless we ask. We must work as "changeologists" and be on constant lookout for evidence of change (Bertolino, 1999).

In the event that a youth, parent, social worker, or other is unsure as to what constitutes change, it can be helpful to suggest examples of change. One possibility is to offer multiple choice questions, such as "Will she be doing _____ or _____ or _____?" The person(s) can either select one of the choices offered or come up with a different description altogether (Bertolino, 1999).

Scaling and Percentage Questions

During intake assessments, it also can be helpful to ask scaling or percentage-based questions (Berg and de Shazer, 1993; Berg and Miller, 1992; de Shazer, 1991, 1994; Lipchik, 1988). Such questions help to indicate incremental or quantitative change. The RYCW asks each person to rate, on a scale of one to ten, the intensity of the complaint. Here's one way to ask this:

> On a scale of one to ten, with one being the worst this problem has ever been and ten being the best things could ever be, how would you rate the problem today?

Once a number has been given, the RYCW encourages the use of action-based language to translate the number into behavioral terms. For example, if a parent responds with the number three, an RYCW would ask, "What is currently happening that indicates to you the situation is a three?" The next step would be to inquire as to what level the parent believes would indicate that sufficient change had occurred. If the same parent responds with an eight, the RYCW could ask through action-based language what would constitute an eight.

For the purposes of residential placement, it's often helpful to inquire as to what number would indicate a successful placement. The RYCW can then help the parent, youth, and others to determine signs that movement is being made toward that identified number,

Bob (Bertolino, 1999) wrote about this process in a previous publication:

> It's also important to determine what will constitute "inbetween" change. That is, what will indicate to the parent or other that progress is being made toward the end goal. For example, if a youth is at a three and the desired outcome is an eight, the RYCW might inquire as to what it will take to get to a three and a half or four. We're aiming for small changes that will indicate that progress is being made.

Percentage questions are similar to scaling questions. To use these questions, the RYCW inquires as to what percentage of the time things are manageable. This is followed by, "What percentage of the time would things need to be going well or manageable for you to feel that things are on track?" Again, action-based language is used and emphasis is given to identifying in-between change.

Initial, face-to-face assessments are an opportunity to get placements off to a good start. By using collaborative, competency-based language, RYCWs can help to create an atmosphere conducive to hope and possibilities and, most important, change.

HOTLINE CALLS AND PHONE ASSESSMENTS

In some residential facilities and, in particular, emergency shelters serving youth and families, the initial contact is through phone calls from parents/legal guardians, court personnel, and social services representatives. For example, at Bob's agency, RYCWs answer a twenty-four-hour hotline, do crisis management, make referrals, and set up intake assessments to determine whether a youth is appropriate for the facility.

Residential facilities typically will have preestablished criteria regarding what information is to be gathered during hotline/phone assessment calls. Information is transferred to hotline forms that are designed to gather information and statistics that are necessary to justify the need for services and satisfy state licensing requirements, grants, and funding sources. An example of a hotline/phone assessment form is offered in Table 3.2. Historically, these forms are problem

TABLE 3.2. Phone Assessment Form

PHONE ASSESSMENT (HOTLINE) FORM

Date:_____ Time:_____ ☐ Walk-in ☐ Phone Call

Call Received by:_____

Name of Youth:_____ DOB:_____ Age:_____

Address:_____ Sex:_____ Race:_____

City:_____ State:_____ Zip Code:_____

Phone Number (with Area Code):_____

Call Placed by:_____

Status Offense: (yes/no) (Check all that apply and give details during summary)
  Runaway_____ Truancy_____ Curfew_____ Alcohol/Drug_____ Incorrigible_____

Abuse/Neglect: (yes/no) (Check all that apply and give details during summary)
  Physical_____ Sexual_____ Emotional_____ Neglect_____
  Recent (within past year)_____ Prior History_____

Additional Information: (Check all that apply and give details during summary)
  Psychiatric History_____ Prior Hospitalizations_____ Prior Placement_____
  Evaluation/Diagnosis_____ Psychotropic Medications_____
  Suicide/Homicide History_____ Aggressive Tendencies (toward whom)_____

Any Medical Problems:
_____
_____

Date of Last Physical:_____ **Last School Attended:**_____

Referred by: (Check one box)
☐ Mental Health Professional   ☐ Department of Mental Health   ☐ Police
☐ Family/Juvenile Court   ☐ School   ☐ Other Agency
☐ Division of Social Services   ☐ Other Agency Program

Name of Referral Source:_____

Response to Call: Intake Assessment Time_____
  Hotline Call Placed_____   Reason Refused Placement_____
  Referred to_____   _____
  _____   _____

(See Reverse Side for Written Summary with Details)

focused and reflective of a residential program's overall approach to working with youth.

Similar to face-to-face assessments, RYCWs may be required to gather specific information during initial phone assessments. We also see this as an opportunity to begin to do three things:

1. Let the person making the hotline call tell his or her story.
2. Begin to use collaborative, competency-based conversations through the use of questioning (refer back to Table 2.3).
3. Get clear on what is the caller's concern or complaint.

The Role of Questioning: Exploring Possibilities Through Phone Assessments

As previously discussed with face-to-face assessments, during phone assessments, oftentimes, RYCWs will be required to ask routine questions that are pathology and problem focused. However, typically there is room for the RYCW to slightly expand the phone conversation and ask more competency-based questions. Let's refer back to Table 3.1 to explore this further.

Take a moment to view the category of status offenses. Status offenses are behaviors that are unlawful for youth, even though they are legal for adults. These generally include breaking curfew, truancy, running away, alcohol possession, and incorrigibility (disobedience). First, for the purposes of agency requirements, an RYCW might inquire about a youth's history of status offenses. A parent might respond, "He's run away six times in three months." The RYCW could then ask, "What was he doing so that he didn't run way more often?" or "How did he do with running away during the three previous months?"

The idea is to begin to explore times when the problem is less oppressive and dominating in the youth's life. When we can inject the element of possibility into our initial phone assessments, we can simultaneously promote hope and, ultimately, the change process. The following is an extended dialogue between a parent trying to place her daughter and an RYCW who has taken the hotline call. The RYCW gains information about the complaint while using collaborative, competency-based conversations to open up possibilities for change:

RYCW: Hello, Youth Services Center. Can I help you?

Parent: Yeah, my son is out of control. I can't handle him anymore. No one can.

RYCW: Okay, your sense is that you can't handle him. Can you tell me what you mean when you say that he's out of control?

Parent: Well, he won't do anything that I ask. He just does what he wants when he wants. He won't go by any rules.

RYCW: What specifically has he done that tells you that he's out of control?

Parent: Last week he skipped three days in a row. The school won't do anything, so what am I supposed to do? And he's failing three of his classes.

RYCW: Okay. He skipped school and he's doing poorly in three of his classes. That gives me an idea. Anything else?

Parent: That's really it, but he just won't listen. It's frustrating.

RYCW: Okay. It seems like he won't listen. I can see why that's frustrating. Is it okay if I ask you a few questions about what you've said so far?

Parent: Sure.

RYCW: You mentioned that he skipped three days in a row of school last week. How come he didn't just skip them all?

Parent: I'm not sure. I mean, he's never even skipped before.

RYCW: So that was out of the ordinary for him?

Parent: Yeah.

RYCW: What about this week?

Parent: He's gone [to school] every day.

RYCW: Really? I wonder how that came about. What do you make of that—that he went every day this week?

Parent: I guess maybe last week was just a bad one. I don't know.

RYCW: Okay. You also mentioned that he's failing three of his classes at school.

Parent: That's right. He used to be at least a B student.

RYCW: What are the grades in his other classes?

Parent: He's got two Cs in science and history and a B-minus in gym.

RYCW: I'm curious. What do you suppose he's doing in those other classes that's helping him to keep his head above water?

Parent: I think he does the work.

Again, our aim is to explore "What else?" during phone assessments. Even when we are working with social services workers, juvenile officers, or others who place youth, we can explore exceptions to the problematic behavior.

It is important to gain clarification from people about what they expect from residential placement. Interestingly, when collaborative, competency-based language is used to open up possibilities, some parents, for example, will shift their views such that other alternatives to placement are considered. They may choose to try outpatient therapy first, for example. In the event that a parent, guardian, or other wants to move to the next step of setting up a face-to-face assessment, the initial phone assessment, we believe, can set a positive tone for the intake interview and, perhaps, for an entire placement.

In the next chapter, we'll explore ways of introducing collaborative, competency-based language into team meetings and staffings, treatment planning, and level systems.

Chapter 4

We're in This Together: Teaming Up in the Service of Change

Do not be too timid and squeamish about your actions. All life is an experiment.

Ralph Waldo Emerson

Most residential facilities incorporate what is known as a *team approach*. Individuals on residential treatment teams hold positions such as social worker, therapist, recreation therapist, music therapist, art therapist, treatment coordinator, psychologist, psychiatrist, and, of course, RYCW. Each team is unique in that it consists of a variety of personalities and each person holds personal views about change, his or her role on the team, and the nature of problems.

It is common on residential teams for some staff members to align with one another and for dominant views about change and the nature of problems to emerge. Due largely to the training and education each team member has received, a predominant language often arises when discussing psychiatric diagnoses, behavior, and the proverbial "big picture." Therein lies a challenge for the RYCW who wishes to incorporate a collaborative, competency-based approach into his or her contribution to the team.

In this chapter, we will broadly discuss the nature and functions of teams in facilities where RYCWs work. We'll also discuss the ways that collaborative, competency-based language can be used in these meetings to open possibilities for youth. Last, we'll delve into how to cocreate realistic and solvable problems with youth and co-workers and discuss ways of working within preestablished level systems.

CREATING CHANGE THROUGH TEAM MEETINGS
AND STAFFINGS

Mark Krueger (1990) defines teamwork as "a process in which team members convene on a regular basis to design, discuss plans for implementing and evaluate individual treatment plans, and coordinate activities for an assigned group of children and families" (p. 124). Team meetings or staffings are generally held once a week, and all staff members are required to attend. These meetings provide a context in which observations and feedback are offered and ideas can be generated to determine effective ways of working with youth.

The overall goal of residential staffings is to ensure that a youth is receiving the highest quality of care and is getting his or her needs met. Therefore, continual evaluation of what is working and what is not is essential. Despite serving as forums for promoting and facilitating change, team meetings can sometimes become "bitch sessions." This happens when a staff member expresses his or her feelings about a particular youth by focusing only on negative behaviors. This is sometimes followed by, in rapid fashion, negative comments from other staff members.

The risk of allowing a team meeting to become too negative in tone is that we don't want to allow a landslide or snowball effect to occur. This is when other staff members pile on the bandwagon of negativity and then the focus becomes one of getting a youth out of a program or completely redesigning an otherwise effective treatment plan. To get an idea of what we are talking about, we provide the following example of how negativity can have a domino or snowball effect in a team meeting:

> **Therapist:** Okay. Let's talk about Joey. What have things been like in the house?
>
> **RYCW #1:** He's been fine on my shifts. He's got a great sense of humor. Sometimes he needs redirection because he doesn't want to do his assignments at night, but I can usually get him to after we talk about it.
>
> **Therapist:** That's great! What else have you noticed?
>
> **RYCW #2:** He really picks on the other kids. He's really mean and I don't think that's right.

Therapist: Can you say more about that?

RYCW #2: He just says stuff and I can't get him to stop. He runs the house when he wants to. [Looks to another RYCW] Karen, you've seen it too.

RYCW #3: Yeah. He does run the house, and he doesn't respond to redirection. He does whatever he wants whenever he wants.

RYCW #4: I agree, and I don't think we're doing any good with him. He needs a more structured program, I think.

RYCW #2: Me too.

In this case, a therapist asked a question that was initially followed by a positive response by an RYCW. However, one not so favorable response spawned a flurry of other comments that created a climate of negativity. In our experience, the tone of a meeting can shift in a matter of just a few seconds. It takes only one convincing person to begin to sway others toward his or her perspective. The focus then becomes one of "what's wrong" versus "what's right."

Diffusing Negativity in Staffings Through Acknowledgment and Possibility

From a collaborative, competency-based perspective, residential staffings provide an avenue to identify and amplify possibilities in the service of change. Yet, we must keep in mind that each staff person brings to team meetings a valid view of the world. To confront negative views is to say to a person, "Your reality is wrong." This is precisely what we don't do. Instead, we acknowledge each staff person's view as valid. We then move to open up possibilities through language.

To do this, we listen diligently to each person's view or story and then begin to "paint doorways in corners" by using the ideas offered in Chapter 3. Here's an example:

RYCW #1: He's always getting into arguments with me about what he's supposed to be doing. He's not getting any better.

RYCW #2: So he's argued with you at times, and your sense is he isn't changing.

RYCW #1: That's right.

All we are trying to do is acknowledge each person's view and introduce the idea that possibilities exist within the problem description. Acknowledgment and validation are the keys to diffusing problem-saturated views and for opening up possibilities. They can neutralize negativity so that the team can work together to generate ideas for creating change. If a staff member does not feel heard, acknowledged, and validated, then it is unlikely that he or she will buy into any new ideas that are generated.

Tapping into the Essential Qualities of Staff Members

When I (Bob) was hired for my first job in the field of mental health, it was for the position of RYCW in an emergency shelter for runaway and homeless youth. When I entered the building for the interview, I saw a youth sitting all alone playing a badly tuned guitar. Being a musician, I offered to tune it for him. Soon I was teaching him chords and songs. I didn't think much of it because I would have done that for anyone. Much later, I was told by the shelter coordinator that one of the reasons I was hired was because even though I was young and needed to learn more, she knew that I could find a way to connect with the youth who stayed in the shelter.

Our contention is that every member of a treatment team brings to a setting particular abilities, competencies, and strengths that help him or her to be effective and to connect with youth. We want to consider the ways that we can tap into each person's individual resources. For example, if a certain staff member seems to relate well with youth who are from inner-city areas, we might want to explore how that staff member could be used to facilitate change with youth from such settings. Or, if a staff member seems to be especially adept at crisis intervention, then we want to find out what it is that he or she does that seems to contribute to him or her being a calming influence on youth.

What we are talking about is finding out what each staff member does well and tapping into those resources. Oftentimes, staff members aren't aware that they are good at something in a residential placement because they use their abilities automatically. That is, they just do what comes naturally or what they've learned without much thought. Yet, as we mentioned, each staff person will have areas of expertise and also areas in which they will need to grow and develop.

In Table 4.1 we've outlined some questions for determining what each staff person does well that can be an asset in residential placements. Table 4.2 will help RYCWs to keep track of weekly successes and identify personal goals.

Treatment Planning, Goal Setting, and Exploring Possibilities in Staffings

Treating planning is part of most residential staffings. This process involves outlining the goals of treatment or placement. It is commonplace in residential placements for therapists, social workers, psychologists, or psychiatrists to be the overall coordinators in treatment planning. Yet, it is generally up to RYCWs to implement the treatment plan. Thus, from a collaborative, competency-based perspective, the voices of RYCWs are important in the treatment planning process.

TABLE 4.1. Questions to Determine Strengths

THE RYCW STRENGTH LIST
1. What assets, abilities, strengths, and resources do you bring to this setting that you believe make you a good RYCW?
2. In what ways might you use those qualities which you identified in the first question in your job as an RYCW?
3. In what ways have you dealt with adversity in the past?
4. How can that be helpful to you in your job as an RYCW?

TABLE 4.2. Form for Recording Successes and Goals

WEEKLY SUCCESS CHART
Name
(name of RYCW)
"Exceptional Work This Week"
(comments written by peers during this week, as well as by the staff member concerned)
Goals
(where the staff member wants to be next week at this time—described in specific, behavioral terms [action talk] in relation to particular youth; this encourages peers to notice times when the staff member achieves this goal)

Copyright © 1992 Linda Metcalf. Slightly modified. Reproduced with permission.

What Are We Doing Here?

Just as with initial assessments, RYCWs want to gain a clear vision, in action-based language, of what needs to change and what will constitute movement in the direction of the desired change. So, as we hear the psychosocial histories of youth, as RYCWs, we want to ask questions that require others to clarify what needs to change. From this perspective, we are not striving for personality transformation or complete cognitive restructuring. We abide by the idea that "if it's not broken, don't fix it" (de Shazer, 1985). Instead, we want to outline concrete goals that address specific behaviors that are posing difficulties for a youth or a family.

Table 4.3 offers some questions that may help to guide RYCWs and other mental health professionals toward clarity in staffings and treatment planning.

Using Action-Based Language to Create Goals

As mentioned earlier, it is important that each staff member has a clear idea of what needs to change (goal) and what that change will look like as it happens. So when an RYCW or other states that depression ought to be a treatment goal for a youth, we ask, "When you say depression, what do you see him or her doing that tells you that he or she is depressed?" We want to get as specific as possible by using action-based language to gain a behavioral description of the complaint, concern, or problem. Videotalk also can be a helpful vehicle in defining change.

TABLE 4.3. Questions to Guide Treatment Planning

RESIDENTIAL STAFFING TREATMENT PLANNING
(Use action-based language for each response.)
1. What led to this youth being placed?
2. Who placed the youth?
3. What are the goals of the parent/legal guardian?
4. What will signify to the parent/legal guardian that the placement has been successful?
5. What does the youth want (goals)?
6. What will signify to the youth that the placement has been helpful?
7. What will be different for the youth and/or family as a result of change?
8. What strengths, abilities, and resources does the youth and/or his or her family bring that may be helpful in resolving the current complaint(s)?
9. How has the youth and/or how have family members dealt with this type of situation or similar difficulties in the past?
10. Is there anything that is currently happening with the youth and/or family that might indicate that change in the desired direction is already happening?
11. What specifically can each member of the treatment team do to facilitate the change process?
12. What specifically will members of the treatment team be watching for that will indicate that progress is being made toward the defined goals?

It also is important to remember that whatever the established goals are, they must be "doable." They must not only be realistic but also attainable. Let's explore how a conversation at a residential staffing might transpire with action-based language being used for goal setting and treatment planning:

RYCW #1: I think that Kelly needs to work on her social skills. She gets scapegoated a lot by the other residents.

RYCW #2: I agree. She really sets herself up with others.

RYCW #3: Okay, so you both feel that Kelly needs to work on her social skills. Can you be more specific and tell me what you've observed that tells you that we should list that as a goal?

RYCW #2: Well, she tries to get the other residents' attention by making weird noises and doing strange things instead of just going up and talking to them. Take yesterday, for instance. Two of the girls were sitting and watching TV and she came into the room and started doing this weird dance to get their attention. They told her to knock it off, and they got so mad they finally left. Then Kelly left the room crying, saying that everyone hated her.

RYCW #3: Okay, so a concern might be how she goes about making friends and interacting with the other residents. Is that right?

RYCW #2: Yeah.

Whereas working on social skills is a very broad, nondescriptive goal, interacting with others is more specific. Again, it is important for everyone to be clear about what needs to change. However, let's remember that there are no wrong ways to view a situation. There are only views. Thus, we want to acknowledge, validate, and value each person's view. At the same time, we can work to gain clarity on what needs change and explore those views which offer possibilities for change.

Occasionally, all parties will not agree on what constitutes better in terms of setting goals. For instance, the unit manager may want the youth to improve in all areas of the program at once. Meanwhile, one RYCW may feel that treatment is successful when the youth improves his or her behavior during morning routine and at bedtime. Most of the time, further negotiations will help the RYCW to gain clarification.

If dissension persists regarding what will constitute positive goals, it is important to recall that residential placement is not about complete personality transformation or psychological reprogramming. That is, our aim is not to change the entire "being" of a youth. We want to remain focused on those aspects which seem to keep youth "stuck." We ask, "What will help this particular youth to move on?" Table 4.4 offers some ideas for ferreting out what constitutes the goals of placement when a lack of agreement exists.

Searching for Exceptions

In residential staffings, we also want to explore other times when maybe the situation is slightly different and the concern is less dominating in the youth's life. At times, the youth or others may have some influence over the problem. To find out about these aspects, we search for exceptions. Here's one way to do this:

TABLE 4.4. Questions That Clarify Goals

CLARIFYING GOALS IN RESIDENTIAL TREATMENT
• What is happening with the youth such that he or she has been placed residentially?
• Who is complaining the most?
• Who is pushing for change?
• Who is alarmed about something?
• What are they complaining or alarmed about (translate vague and blaming words into action description—use action/videotalk)?
• Who is willing to pay for the placement and/or do something to effect change?
• Whose concerns will constrain or affect placement?
• Who will be able to terminate the placement?
• What are the legal and ethical restraints or considerations (suicide plans/ attempts, homicide and violence plans/history, court/legal involvement, etc.)?

RYCW #3: So, can someone tell me about times when Kelly seems to make friends with other residents and how her methods of interacting work for her?

RYCW #2: You know, she really gets along well with Amanda and Kim. They tolerate her more and actually think she's funny sometimes.

RYCW #3: Really? How does that happen?

RYCW #2: I'm not sure, but she doesn't always act inappropriately around others.

RYCW #1: That's true—just sometimes.

RYCW #3: Okay. So, sometimes the way she approaches others works for her and sometimes it doesn't. We'd like to help her become more successful at making friends and at interacting with others in ways that work for her. Is that what we want?

RYCWs: Yes.

Part of the day-to-day ritual of residential programming involves staff searching for as many opportunities to respond to even the smallest signs that residents are achieving success or are taking steps forward. We *assume* that there will be many examples of success—that there will be many exceptions to problematic behavior. Residential staffings provide a context to help RYCWs and others orient toward searching for possibilities and change, as opposed to the traditional idea of discovering and uncovering deficits and signs of pathology. With this in mind, incremental or small instances of change ought to be outlined in staffings. That is, what will the youth be doing along the way that will indicate to others that he or she is moving in the direction of the goal?

What Will Change Look Like?

Another consideration to investigate during staffings is what the change will look like once it begins to happen (and this may show, as with Kelly, that it already is happening to some degree). This orients RYCWs and others to what is happening that is right with a youth. Here's one way to inquire about this:

RYCW #3: What will it look like when Kelly is interacting with others a little better than she is now?

RYCW #2: She'll have more friends, for one. Things will be calmer too. There won't be as many eruptions between her and the other residents.

RYCW #1: I think she'll feel better about herself.

RYCW #3: How will you know when she's feeling better about herself? What will she be doing?

RYCW #1: She'll be making more eye contact—as she used to do—and she'll be smiling more.

RYCW #3: So there will be several signs that Kelly is interacting better with others.

By being "exception seekers," we can search for the moments when youth are doing those behaviors which are moving them toward established goals. In this way, it is not necessary that RYCWs "teach" all desired behaviors, as they may already exist within the youth's experience. Our task becomes one of evoking those moments of competence and ability.

Hearing the Voices of Youth

Residential staffings and treatment planning in general preclude the voices of youth. This is an interesting phenomenon. Why is this so? This is, in part, due to the fact that mental health professionals are viewed as experts on the lives of others; it is assumed that they can *know* the truth about what's going on with, and what is best for, youth.

Ben Furman and Tapani Ahola (1992) have discussed how they have included clients in their case staffings as a way to involve them in the treatment planning process. We think along the same lines as Furman and Ahola in regard to youth; yet, for a variety of reasons, most residential facilities will not allow youth to attend staffings and treatment planning sessions. Thus, we have devised a form that youth can fill out for use in staffings so that they may, in some way, have their voices heard (see Table 4.5). The form allows youth a forum to bring to light those things which they feel staff members should know about when treatment planning.

TABLE 4.5. Form for Youth to Send to Planning Sessions

WHAT STAFF SHOULD KNOW ABOUT ME
Name: _____ Date: _____ Age:_____
1. Things that I want to accomplish while I'm here (what I want to work on):
2. What I need staff to know about me:
3. What I want for myself in the future:
4. Things that I am good at:
5. What I need from staff:
6. People who believe in me:
Signed:_____

Using a collaborative, competency-based approach requires RYCWs and others to think about the ways in which youth can be involved in all phases of placement. This not only is respectful consideration; it also allows room for multiple perspectives to be considered. We consider it a gift when a youth shares with us his or her ideas and theories about change.

IT'S YOUR TURN: THE PROCESS OF CHANGING SHIFTS

Most facilities schedule a brief meeting when one group of workers takes over for another. These usually last for just a few minutes, as the departing members of one shift tell those coming on shift what actions they should consider, what shape the kids are in, and what kind of day it was (Crone, 1984). We view shift changes as an excellent opportunity to

1. discuss problematic areas or situations, including what staff did that didn't work, what did work (including partial successes), and what might work in the future—vital information for oncoming staff;
2. discuss what staff did that made a positive difference during the previous shift; and
3. set a tone that enables exceptions and possibilities that were noted on the previous shift to be identified, punctuated, and amplified during the next shift.

Also, some particular questions can help incoming RYCWs determine what has gone right during a shift. Here are some possible questions:

• What did you notice happening during your shift that you'd like to have continue into other shifts?
• What kinds of things did you notice each resident doing that might be an indication that he or she is moving toward his or her goals?
• What were the highlights of your shift in regard to the residents?
• What specifically did you do to help the situation remain manageable?

By asking questions such as these, RYCWs can obtain important information and simultaneously become more oriented toward creating change, as opposed to "putting out fires." Although there often is little time for extensive conversation between RYCWs—both coming and going—these interchanges can be brief. In addition, RYCWs can choose which areas are most important to address during shift change, therefore using those questions which are most applicable.

I'm Fried; I'm Out of Here: When Frustration Sets In

During shift changes, RYCWs tend to make comments such as "Everything was great! See ya" or "Good luck! They're all yours!" These comments tell incoming RYCWs relatively little about events of the previous shift. Further, if it's been a particularly rough shift, the departing RYCWs may want to move along as quickly as possible. In other cases, they may remain long enough to give the "lowdown." In the latter, the soon to be off-shift RYCWs let the soon to be on-shift RYCWs know "what they are in for."

When a changeover only seems to be a revelation of bad news, oncoming RYCWs must beware of being hypnotized into problem-saturated views. There may be concerns and physical realities to deal with on a shift (e.g., residents fighting, an incident of stealing, etc.); however, fact can easily lead to problematic stories when RYCWs are frustrated, tired, and so forth. We must remember that the RYCW's job can be difficult and often exhausting. Thus, our first move is to acknowledge and validate those RYCWs who are coming off shift. At the same time, we use possibility-laced language to become clear about what actions and behaviors occurred on a shift. Here's an example of how to do this:

RYCW #1: I'm glad you're here. It's been a rough night.

RYCW #2: What happened?

RYCW #1: All of the kids were acting up. It was nuts. I'm exhausted. I can't wait to get out of here.

RYCW #2: I can see that you're tired. Can I just ask you a couple of questions so that I'm clear about how things have been?

RYCW #1: Sure.

RYCW #2: Thanks. I'll be brief. So it seemed to you that all of the kids were acting up.

RYCW #1: Well, I guess it wasn't all of them. It just seemed like it because it was so chaotic.

RYCW #2: Yeah, I've had a few shifts like that too. So who was doing what, specifically?

RYCW #1: It was really Jeff, Alex, and Rob. Jeff and Alex had a loud shouting match, and Rob was egging them on by calling them names.

RYCW #2: That must have been tough. What did you do?

RYCW #1: I was able to get Rob's attention and have him leave the room, and then they just said a few more words and seemed to calm down.

RYCW #2: Good job. That was a great idea.

It's important that RYCWs get clear action descriptions of problematic behaviors during changeovers. In addition, when information can be obtained about ideas, interventions, or approaches that might have worked with various youth, RYCWs can be better prepared to work with a myriad of situations that may arise on shift. As discussed earlier, it's generally helpful to know what didn't work, what did work, and what might work in the future.

Another way of working toward a smooth transition during changeover is to use a shift change form. Table 4.6 offers an example of how to orient RYCWs toward what didn't work, what did work to any degree, and what might work during upcoming shifts. Since most facilities have at least two RYCWs on duty at all times, it's also an opportunity for staff to collaboratively concur about the details of a shift. Using this type of form may be especially helpful in facilities where shift changes are extremely brief, yet there is much information to pass on.

Checking in with Youth

Following shift change and attention to immediate duties, it is common for RYCWs to check in with the youth in their facilities. Since we are working as changeologists, these interactions are seen as excellent opportunities to inquire about differences, exceptions, and change. There are many possibilities in terms of finding out about change. Here is one example of how an RYCW might talk with a youth and search for change:

RYCW: Hi, Sally. How have you been?

Sally: Okay I guess. But Sharon better back off or she's gonna get it.

RYCW: What's bothering you about Sharon?

Sally: She's getting on my nerves. She keeps talking about me behind my back.

RYCW: So you feel that maybe she's said things about you. I'm sorry if that's happening. I'm curious though, how have you managed to keep it together?

Sally: I just say that she's not worth it.

RYCW: That sounds like a great idea. How does telling yourself that help you?

Sally: Because then I remember that it's not worth getting in trouble and I calm down.

Another possibility is to say to youth, "Tell me about what's better since the last time I worked" or "I'd like to hear about all the good things you've been up to since we last saw each other." Such a beginning to the day reflects to youth the assumption that there will be something that is better (Durrant, 1993). Although significant change happens on a regular basis, all we are searching for is small moments of change that may indicate movement in a preferred direction. We can then move to amplify these changes by offering praise and following up with questions such as "How did you do that?" and "How can you do that more often?"

Group and Community Meetings

Most residential programs utilize a variety of meetings to discuss unit issues and rules, learn basic skills, and resolve conflicts. Although these groups can be very therapeutic, they differ from the traditional idea of group therapy. These meetings typically are led by RYCWs, but some programs may allow residents who have reached a certain level to be in charge. It is not uncommon for unit meetings to become problem saturated and confrontational, which often leads those involved to become defensive and critical. Here we offer some ways to use language to diffuse negativity and make these meetings more respectful, collaborative, and competency based.

We have emphasized the importance of creating a respectful climate in our interactions with youth, and the same holds true for group unit meetings. Each resident has a view that is valid and ought

TABLE 4.6. Sample Shift Change Form

SHIFT CHANGE FORM

Staff Member on Duty _____

_____

Date: _____   Time of Shift: _____

1. On a scale of 1 to 10, with 1 being as poor as things could be and 10 being as good as things could be in the program, where would you rate things on your shift? _____

   What was happening to warrant the rating given? _____
   _____
   _____

2. What would need to happen for things to improve ½ point higher than the given rating? _____
   _____

3. What specific things did you or others do that didn't work too well, worked to some degree, or might work in the future? _____
   _____
   _____

4. What did you notice happening during your shift that you would like to have continue to happen during upcoming and future shifts? _____
   _____
   _____

5. What kinds of things did you or others do during the shift to help keep things manageable? _____
   _____
   _____

6. Is there anything else that might be helpful for oncoming staff to know? ____
   _____
   _____

to be heard. At the same time, it's critical that the group leader holds each person accountable for what he or she says and does. To get things off to a good start, here's one way to begin a group:

This group provides an opportunity for each of us to share what we think and feel about what goes on around here. We've got some things that we'd like to talk about with you and you'll be able to talk about any concerns you may have. But, before we get going, there's a couple of things that we have to make sure are clear. First, let's all be respectful of one another. There are lots of ways to look at things and we want to be respectful of one another's ideas, thoughts, and feelings. You don't have to agree with another person, but you need to be respectful. Also, there's no blaming in here. If you have a concern, speak about how it affects you and what you would like to see change. If you're not sure how to bring it up or speak about it without blaming someone, then ask us to help you. It's also important that when a person is talking, we let him or her speak without interruption. Last, we value what you have to say and want to help you in whatever ways that we can to resolve your concerns. To do this, we want to use this group as a forum for not just talking about problems but also for finding solutions to those problems.

We've already discussed different ways that RYCWs can use collaborative, competency-based language to open up possibilities in other contexts. These same conversations also can be used with unit meetings. For example, when a concern is raised, an RYCW will want to gain a clear picture of it. From there, he or she might inquire as to what the situation will look like when things are better. Since there may be many views of the problem, the RYCW will need to acknowledge and validate each viewpoint and work to generate a unified goal. RYCWs can then move to identify in-between change. Here's one way of doing this:

RYCW: Okay, who would like to talk about a concern that he or she has?

James: I would. I'm really pissed off.

RYCW: What's happened that's pissed you off?

James: Some people just need to mind their own business!

RYCW: I don't know what you mean. Can you give an example of what you're talking about?

James: Yeah. Some people say things behind other people's backs.

RYCW: Without naming names, please give us an example so that we can all be clear about what it is that's bothering you.

James: Okay. I told someone something about me that I didn't want anybody else to know and he blabbed it all over.

RYCW: So, it's upsetting to you that you told someone something in confidence and that person, as far as you know, spoke about it to someone else?

MIKE: I know he's talking about me!

RYCW: Mike, we want to hear what you have to say because it's important, and you'll get a chance to speak in a moment. But right now it's James's turn. [Looks at James] First, let me say that I'm sorry if that happened to you. What do you think needs to happen here so that you can begin to feel better about what you've experienced?

James: I don't know.

RYCW: Okay. You're not real clear what you want to have happen, but you know that it's upsetting to you—and you want everyone to know how you feel.

James: Yeah.

RYCW: Okay. If you want to talk about it later, I'll be available, or you can meet with another staff member. Is that okay?

James: Yeah.

Again, it's important to understand what the youth's concern is and where he or she wants to go from there. Sometimes a youth just needs to be heard and that will be enough. Other times, more specific action will need to be taken.

When there aren't any specific concerns to discuss, it can be helpful to orient the group members toward the prospects of change through "process groups." Table 4.7 offers a chart that RYCWs can use to identify small goals and to highlight successes and changes that may indicate movement in the direction of larger or more long-term goals.

TABLE 4.7. Forms for Guiding Process Groups

MORNING/EVENING PROCESS GROUPS

A.M. Process Group

Date: _____

Goal for Today: _____

1. How have you accomplished this goal a little bit or a lot in the past?

2. How were you wise enough to accomplish it in this way?

3. Of these strategies you have used before, which one will you use today?

4. On a scale of 1 to 10 (with 1 being completely impossible and 10 being completely successful), where would you like to be at the end of the day?

P.M. Process Group

5. On the scale in question #4, how close did you get to achieving your goal? How did you do that?

6. Ask your group members what changes they noticed in you today as you moved toward your goal.

Here are some other questions that can facilitate conversation in process groups:

- What's been better since the last unit/community meeting?
- What have you noticed happening that you'd like to have continue?
- What's one small change that might make things better for all of you as a group?
- Who here, do you think, has made the most positive change since the last meeting?

Unit and community groups are an excellent medium for identifying and promoting change. They also provide an opportunity for RYCWs to model various ways of resolving conflicts.

THOUGHTS ON LEVEL SYSTEMS

As discussed in our overview of residential youth care work (see the preface), behavioral orientations in residential treatment continue to be the standard. In fact, most facilities use behaviorally oriented level systems to help the team and the youth keep track of the youth's progress. Level systems generally provide clear systems of rewards and consequences and are goal based. They also allow residential teams to adopt a single philosophy for managing behavior.

Level systems typically include "promotions" to higher levels and "demotions" to lower levels. For example, a youth may be promoted from level one to level two because he or she had presented "appropriate" behavior, completed assignments for that level, and been interviewed by a staff member. Conversely, a level demotion may be the consequence for a youth who is caught smoking in one of the unit bathrooms. Depending on the program philosophy, level changes can be based on team decisions or left up to those who are on duty. The latter can occur when a youth "petitions" for the next level and is interviewed at that time. In some programs, discharge, or "graduation," is contingent on the achievement of a specific level (Durrant, 1993).

A concern with level systems is the implication that change is a one-way street. That is, a youth who is making progress will necessarily change in a positive or upward direction. In actuality, youth more often change in an up-and-down fashion. Thus, Durrant (1993) points out that even though level systems appear to be based on rewarding successful or desired behavior, they may easily contribute to ideas of failure. Setbacks that often are a part of learning may carry a purely negative connotation, even though they may just be part of a youth's process of growing. For youth who have histories of difficulties that have contributed to a sense of failure, this feeling may be reinforced by doing poorly within the framework of a level system.

There is an additional concern with level systems. For some youth, the goal may become to attain a higher level when achieving that level should be just a part of a more successful future (Durrant, 1993). Although residential programs may rely on level systems, it is crucial that RYCWS understand that change is not a one-directional process *and* level promotions are but one indicator that progress is being made.

Given this, within preestablished level systems, to foster further change, open possibilities, and punctuate the strengths and competencies of youth, there are some questions that RYCWs can consider that serve to highlight small indicators of change, such as the following:

- What kinds of things have you been doing to move toward your goals?
- What are you doing to keep yourself going in the right direction?
- How did you manage to complete four out of the five tasks you outlined for today?
- How did you manage to earn 250 out of 400 points today?
- What will it take to keep that going?
- What will you be doing to earn 275 points?
- How did you keep from losing more than forty points?
- How will others know that you're ready to be promoted to the next level?

"Petitioning" for Promotion to Higher Levels

When youth are petitioning to move to higher levels, some residential programs will require that a form be filled out to identify change that has occurred. We've included a form that can help to identify the progress of youth (see Table 4.8).

Within preestablished level systems, RYCWs can use collaborative, competency-based language to create change. In the next two chapters, we'll explore more specific ways of changing unhelpful patterns of action and interaction, views, and aspects of context. These ideas can be used within level systems and within all aspects of residential placement.

TABLE 4.8. Level Promotion Petition Form That Identifies Progress

LEVEL PROMOTION PETITION FORM
Name:_____   Date: _____
From Level _____   to   _____ Interviewed By: _____
Please list five things that you like about yourself. 1. 2. 3. 4. 5. Please list three goals that you have accomplished while in this program. 1. 2. 3. Please list three goals that you will be working on in the future. 1. 2. 3. Please explain what you think staff should consider when reviewing your petition.   _____ Signature of youth

Chapter 5

Now You See It, Now You Don't: Altering Problematic Patterns of Viewing

If you are distressed by anything external, the pain is not due to the thing itself, but to your estimate of it; and, this you have the power to revoke at any moment.

Marcus Aurelius

THE ROLE OF VIEWS

The views that youth and others associated with youth subscribe to can engender or suppress hope. Some views are validating, open up possibilities, and move youth toward future goals. Others are invalidating and inhibit and close down pathways with possibilities. When troubling problems develop with youth in residential treatment (as well as in other contexts), oftentimes it's due to unhelpful views. Views typically come in two forms—*attentional patterns* and *stories*. Attentional patterns typically find youth or others focusing on certain aspects of a youth's life. Stories represent how youth or others have come to describe their perceptions over time.

As discussed previously, what youth experience internally is all okay and should be acknowledged and validated; however, the attentional patterns and stories that they, as well as others, subscribe to may be unhelpful at times. Thus, attentional patterns and stories that are hopeful and leave open possibilities for change should be promoted and those which close down avenues of change should be challenged (Bertolino, 1999).

To get a clearer picture of the role that views play and the influence that RYCWs can have on these in residential settings, we'll first discuss attentional patterns and then move to the realm of stories.

Problematic Attentional Patterns

An RYCW in an emergency shelter for youth had been struggling with a female resident, Stacy. During supervision, the RYCW stated that Stacy was "being manipulative and sneaky," as she had on a regular basis noticed her "hanging around the staff office and avoiding her chores and homework." Following these situations, the RYCW would confront Stacy and arguments would ensue, sometimes ending with Stacy crying hysterically. As the supervisor and the RYCW talked, the supervisor wondered aloud if maybe Stacy was hanging around the staff office for other reasons. The supervisor suggested that the RYCW consider some other hypotheses about Stacy before concluding that she was being manipulative and sneaky. She was to report back to the supervisor in one week.

One week later, the RYCW returned to supervision. She told her supervisor that she had been thinking about Stacy's behavior and thought that maybe hanging around the staff office was giving the youth a sense of comfort in some way. The supervisor asked what she might do differently based on that view. The RYCW stated that she would acknowledge the fact that Stacy liked hanging out with staff but that there was a time to do that and a time to do her work. The supervisor suggested that the RYCW see how this view panned out on the unit. With her new view in tow, the RYCW approached Stacy differently than in previous encounters. To her surprise, the RYCW was able to get Stacy to do her work without further provocation.

The implications of problematic patterns of attention are twofold for RYCWs. First, as with the previous scenario, RYCWs have their own views that can be problematic and lead to unhelpful patterns of acting and interacting. In these cases, a change in perspective for an RYCW may be necessary.

A major league baseball player was having an "all-star" season. He was leading the league in hitting and playing better than he ever had. After the midseason all-star break, he returned to the diamond only to find that he was struggling as a hitter. He couldn't believe that things had changed so quickly. When he continued to slump at the plate, he decided to go back and watch videotape footage of himself hitting in an effort to find out what he was doing wrong. As the player watched tapes of himself striking out and hitting weak ground balls, he noticed that he was pulling off pitches. He also noticed that he was lunging at the ball and that he was moving his feet too much. Soon he was more depressed than before he had watched the tapes, knowing that he had so many things to correct in his batting. As he continued to study the videotapes, the team hitting coach, who was wandering through the corridor, spotted the player.

The coach inquired, "What are you doing?"

"I'm watching tapes of myself to figure out what I'm doing wrong," explained the player.

The coach followed, "Why are you watching yourself strike out and do poorly? You ought to be watching tapes of yourself that show you playing at your best. Watch the ones that show you hitting the ball hard and doing the things you want to do at the plate."

The player said that he hadn't thought of that before and did as the coach suggested. Within a few games, he had his swing back and was on track with his hitting again.

The baseball player was not holding a wrong view, just an unhelpful one. The coach merely suggested that he attend to his concern in a different way. Once the player followed suit, he was able to gain a new perspective, which ultimately contributed to the improvement in his hitting. O'Hanlon and Weiner-Davis (1989) commented that a shift in view "can lead to changes in action and the stimulation of unused potentials and resources" (p. 126). This can be especially helpful for RYCWs, as the generation of a new view can lead to a small shift in an attentional pattern, thereby leading to new and creative ideas for working with youth.

A second implication is that RYCWs must be aware of what youth attend to in their lives. If youth only attend to certain aspects of their lives that seem to barricade them from change, then part of the RYCWs' job becomes one of helping youth to notice those aspects which are different and may help to facilitate change. In short, RYCWs can work with youth to generate new views that lead to new self-perceptions and patterns of acting and interacting.

Problematic or Problem-Saturated Stories

Youth and others develop their perspectives based on who they are, including their past experiences and social interactions. White and Epston (1990) have referred to stories that close down possibilities as being *problem saturated*. That is, when problem-saturated or problematic stories about youth are present, the possibilities of change can seem virtually nonexistent.

The views that youth and others abide by are subject to negotiation and change. They aren't set in stone. When these stories already hold the possibility of change, RYCWs can work with youth so that they can take *action* to facilitate change in the present and in the future (Bertolino, 1999). In contrast, when stories are problematic or possibilities are closed down, RYCWs must first help to negotiate new ways of viewing that are conducive to change.

When Steven Spielberg was a teenager and living in Phoenix, he was a member of the Flaming Arrow Patrol of Ingleside's Troop 294. One of the parents who supervised the boys during this time was a man named Dick Hoffman. Over time, as people do, Hoffman developed an image of the young Spielberg. He described his view of Steven:

> He seemed to go in fits and starts—he would dash from one thing to another. I thought it was a disability, not being able to concentrate the way the rest of us would. I knew he was wildly enthusiastic, but I didn't think he had enough ability to analyze things. . . . I thought, "When he grows up and gets into the real world he's going to have a tough time keeping up." I didn't dream anything would come of him. Of course, that was a complete misjudgment of the kid's personality. (McBride, 1997, pp. 77-78)

A common characteristic of problem-saturated stories is that they all create a mirage or smoke screen for RYCWs. Problematic stories are deceiving in that they appear to be so real that RYCWs and others can become entranced by them. RYCWs can become convinced that what they are observing is the truth. We want to recognize that what actually exists behind these mirages is a youth who is more complex than any one story or narrative. Instead of becoming participants in problematic stories about youth, as RYCWs, we want to challenge or cast doubt upon them and open up possibilities where none seem to exist.

Next we'll discuss how RYCWs can help to change problematic patterns of attention and stories to which youth and others subscribe.

CHANGING PROBLEMATIC PATTERNS OF VIEWING

When youth or others hold unhelpful views, it can be difficult for them to see things from another perspective. Our task, then, is to help youth and others to change the unhelpful views to which they subscribe. Again, this requires that the RYCW consider "What else?" Such a question can lead to a shift in attention or to the creation of a new story that engenders hope and possibility.

Just as RYCWs' views can become closed down, it is common for those who are close to youth to tune in to one or two aspects of a youth or his or her situation because that's what is most noticeable or alarming. From these views, generalizations and problematic stories can be created that may contribute to the stuckness that's being experienced. By helping people to shift attention elsewhere, unhelpful views can be changed. A small shift in perspective can lead to changes in action and behavior. What follows are three ways to challenge or cast doubt on unhelpful patterns of attention and problematic stories (Bertolino, 1999).

Transform the Story by Acknowledging and Adding the Element of Possibility

In Chapter 3, ways that RYCWs can acknowledge what youth experience internally while simultaneously opening up possibilities were offered. Acknowledgment of current or past problematic viewpoints, combined with the element of possibility, can help to reorient youth to different parts or aspects of their lives or situations. Here's an example of how to do this:

> **Youth:** Everybody is mean to me. I'm tired of it.
>
> **RYCW:** It's been difficult for you because in the past, some people treated you poorly.
>
> **Youth:** Yeah. Nobody likes me.
>
> **RYCW:** You've gotten the idea that people don't like you.
>
> **Youth:** Yeah.
>
> **RYCW:** And up to this point, most people haven't responded to you in a way that you'd like them to.
>
> **Youth:** Yeah.

By acknowledging this youth's internal experience (frustrated) and then introducing the possibility that change may occur by using statements relating to partiality ("some"), perceptions ("you've gotten the idea"), and past tense ("up to this point," "treated," and "haven't responded"), the problematic view began to be deconstructed. The youth was then open to the possibility of change.

Find Counterevidence

This involves having the youth or others tell you something that doesn't fit with the problematic story. Again, this involves asking, "What else?" To find counterevidence, the RYCW acknowledges all internal experience and then explores other aspects of the youth's life, event, or situation. Here's an example of how counterevidence can play a role in the shifting of views:

> **Youth:** I never do anything right.
>
> **RYCW:** Your sense is that there have been times that you haven't done things right. Can you give me an example?

Youth: I keep getting in trouble because I can't remember to do my level assignments.

RYCW: So you've been in some trouble because sometimes you've forgotten to do your level assignments. When was the most recent time that you were able to complete part of one of your level assignments?

Youth: Last week I did them all, but this week I only did a few.

RYCW: Really! Last week you did all of them? How did you do that?

Youth: I just sat at the table until I was done.

The problematic story and view presented by the youth was that he "never" did anything right. The RYCW acknowledged his concern while introducing possibility language, including using statements to reflect perceptions ("your sense is"), past tense ("haven't done"), and partiality ("sometimes"). Then, the RYCW began to search for counterevidence that might dispute the problematic story and lead to a change in perspective.

To find counterevidence, we suggest beginning in the present and working backward. The reason for this is the more current the evidence, the stronger it will be. Sometimes an RYCW may have to go back a few months, a year, or even a few years to find evidence that contradicts the problematic story. That's okay. Evidence is evidence.

As mentioned earlier, in our experience, it's generally easier to evoke or elicit past abilities and competencies than to teach youth something they've never done. For example, if a youth is trying to resolve a conflict (which nearly everyone has done at one time or another), we want to search for times when he or she was successful in that area (to any degree) in the past and then build on it. It's a matter of the RYCW working with the youth to elicit the ability and then applying it to the problem context (Bertolino, 1999). If it's within the youth's experience, it becomes an ability as opposed to a deficit and something that has to be taught. We've found this to be more helpful than trying to teach conflict resolution or anger management or to do assertiveness training.

There's another reason. When RYCWs only teach skills such as those just mentioned, youth and others may only turn to "experts" when future problems arise and downplay or mistrust the significance of their own unique solutions and perspectives (Nylund and Corsiglia, 1994; Smith, 1997; Zimmerman and Dickerson, 1996). Thus, searching for counterevidence relies on evoking and eliciting competency rather than giving youth or others a tool that may or may not work for them, may or may not be used by them, or does not involve their own personal experiences, including abilities, strengths, resources, and solutions (past, present, or future) (Bertolino, 1999).

Find Alternative Stories or Frames That Fit the Same Evidence or Facts

Sometimes a youth or another's interpretation of the youth or other person, event, or situation is closed down and an RYCW's interpretation can offer a different point of view and lead to the dissolution of a problematic story. Specifically, when a youth or other makes a closed-down statement relating to a problematic story, the RYCW can *offer* an alternative story or interpretation. Here's an example:

> **Youth:** My parents don't have a clue how to raise me. All they do is ground me and make my life miserable.

> **RYCW:** It seems to you that their mission is to put restrictions on you and make your life miserable. You know, your parents haven't raised a sixteen-year-old before and you haven't been a sixteen-year-old before. I wonder if maybe your parents are doing what they think is best, and you just haven't educated them yet about what it's like to be a sixteen-year-old in the 1990s.

Again, it is important to use acknowledgment and possibility-laced language in conjunction with an interpretation. In addition, the RYCW introduces any interpretation from a position of *conjecture* or wonderment (Andersen, 1991; Hoffman, 1990; Penn and Sheinberg, 1991). This is done by prefacing questions with phrases such as "I wonder," "Is it possible," or "Could it be." A position of conjecture allows the RYCW to offer alternative views from a position of curiosity, as opposed to stating these views as truth or fact.

A DIFFERENT VIEW: EXTERNALIZING THE PROBLEM

In working with youth, sometimes problematic stories can seem to take on lives of their own. That is, a youth, in his or her own view or in the view of others, *becomes the problem*. For example, instead of expressing troubling behavior, a youth becomes "trouble." The youth is viewed as characterologically flawed or "bad," therefore impairing the youth's *identity* story.

As previously discussed, stories are not set in stone and are changeable. To change problematic or spoiled identity stories, RYCWs want to invite youth into conversations that lead to the reauthoring of alternative and less oppressive stories (Bertolino, 1999, 1998a). In addition to the methods already offered, another way of changing unhelpful stories and views is to use *externalizing* conversations (White and Epston, 1990). These types of conversations help to separate the problem from the youth by determining the problem's influence over the youth. The youth is never considered the problem; the problem is the problem.

Bill O'Hanlon (1994; Rowan and O'Hanlon, 1998) has outlined eight steps that can serve as a guide for RYCWs who are using externalizing conversations. These are outlined in the following material.

Find a Name for the Problem

The RYCW begins by working with the youth to collaboratively come up with a name that fits the problem. Remember, the problem is considered separate from the youth:

> Jarrett had been having difficulty keeping his hands to himself. During a conversation, an RYCW asked him, "What kind of a name do you think we ought to give to this thing that's been giving you trouble?" When Jarrett didn't seem to have an

answer, the RYCW suggested, "You know, it seems as if 'hands all over' is what sometimes happens with you." Jarrett then replied, "Nuh uh, Craig [another RYCW] calls it 'Mr. Happy Hands.' That's what it is."

Sometimes the names that are chosen will begin with Mr., Ms., and so on (e.g., Mr. Tantrum, Ms. Sassy, etc.). This seems to work best with younger youth (Bertolino, 1999). More often, the names that are decided upon are basic descriptions, such as violence, tantrums, aggression, or common psychiatric labels, such as ADHD or conduct disorder.

Personify and Begin to Externalize the Problem

Once the problem has been given a name, the RYCW talks with the youth as if the problem is another person with an identity, will, tactics, and intentions that oppress, undermine, or dominate the youth:

- How long have The Fits been hanging out with you?
- When Mr. Happy Hands whispers in your ears, do you always listen?
- When did The Scream first invite himself over for an extended visit?

Find Out How the Problem Has Dominated, Disrupted, or Undermined the Youth's Life or Relationships

The RYCW explores how the youth has felt dominated or cornered by the problem to do or experience things he or she didn't like. The RYCW can investigate several areas: (1) experience or feelings arising from the influence of the problem; (2) tactics or messages the problem uses to convince youth of limitations or to discourage them; (3) actions or habits the problem invites or encourages the youth to do; (4) speculations about the intentions of the problem in regard to the youth or relationships; and (5) preferences or differences in perspective that the youth has with the problem:

- How has Mr. Happy Hands come between you and others on the unit?

- When has ADHD recruited you into something that you later got in trouble for?
- Why do you think Fighting wants to leave you without any friends?

It is important to notice that the language used is not deterministic. O'Hanlon (1994) stated, "The problem never *causes* or *makes* the family do anything, it only *influences, invites, tells, tries to convince, uses, tricks, tries to recruit*, etc." (p. 26). The youth remains accountable for his or her actions.

Find Moments When Things Went Better or Differently in Regard to the Problem

The RYCW talks with the youth about moments of choice or success that he or she has had in not being dominated or cornered by the problem to do or experience things he or she didn't like. This can spell "bad news" for the problem (Epston, 1997):

- When have you been able to stand up to Mr. Happy Hands?
- When has Temper Tantrums whispered in your ear but you didn't listen?
- Tell me about times when The Fits couldn't convince you to act out.

Use These Moments of Choice or Success As a Gateway to Alternate (Hero/Valued) Stories of Identity

The RYCW encourages the youth to explain what kind of person he or she is that allowed him or her to have those moments of choice or success:

- What qualities do you think you possess that help you to stand up to Mr. Happy Hands' plans for you?
- What is it about you that enabled you to go on strike against Temper Tantrums?
- How do you explain that you are the kind of person that would lodge a protest against ADHD?

Find Evidence from the Youth's Past or Present That Supports the Valued Story

The RYCW searches with the youth for those people, both past and present, who knew (or know) he or she wasn't (isn't) himself or herself when under the influence of the problem. These people could remind the youth of his or her accomplishments, qualities, or resourcefulness. In addition, find out what the youth remembers about his or her life that fits with the valued story rather than the problematic identity story:

- What do you think your teacher from last year would say if she could hear you talk about standing up to The Fits?
- Who is someone who knew you a while back who wouldn't be surprised to hear that you've been able to reject Violence's taunting?
- What can you tell me about yourself that would help me to understand how you've been able to take a stand against Mr. Happy Hands?

Get the Youth to Speculate About a Future That Comes Out of the Valued Story

The RYCW has the youth or other residential staff speculate as to what kinds of changes might occur as he or she continues on a path of resisting the problem:

- As Keith continues standing up to and laughing in the face of The Meanies, how do you think that will affect his family relationships?
- As you continue to maintain the upper hand with The Fits, what do you think will be different about your school life from the one The Fits had planned for you?
- How do you think your strategy with Mr. Happy Hands will help you out in the long run?

Develop a Social Sense of the Valued Story

The RYCW helps the youth to find a real or imagined audience for the changes that have been discussed. The youth also can be enlisted as an expert consultant on solving or standing opposed to the problem:

- What do you think Alice's stance against The Scream has shown you that you wouldn't have otherwise known about her?
- Who needs to know that you've made a commitment to keep Mr. Happy Hands from hanging out without permission?
- Who could benefit from knowing about your enlistment in the Antilying Club?

The steps outlined here are merely a guide for RYCWs who want to learn an alternative way of dialoguing with youth. Once comfortable with externalizing problems, RYCWs can modify this process or create a new one. The following case example (Bertolino, 1999) illustrates the use of externalization with an eleven-year-old youth:

Ray was referred to therapy for being disruptive in class. This included bothering other students so they could not complete their work, walking around the classroom when he was supposed to be seated, making animal noises, and talking back to the teacher. Both Ray's mother and his teacher at school were concerned and wanted to see his behavior change.

Ray was asked, "What do you think we should call this problem?" Initially he seemed puzzled by the question. So he was asked, "Remember the Grinch Who Stole Christmas?" Ray nodded that he did. "At first the Grinch was pushed around by grumpiness. What's pushing you around?" I asked. Ray replied, "My mom says I got ants in my pants." It was agreed that Ants were the problem for Ray.

As the therapy proceeded it was learned that Ants had been around the entire school year, and were convincing Ray that he should get up, move around the classroom and disrupt others. The Ants did this by convincing him that he wouldn't get in trouble. But Ray was upset with this because he felt Ants were lying to him because he kept getting in trouble and missing recess.

Ray and his mother were asked what things would be like when he was no longer being pushed around by Ants. Ray said he'd get to go to recess and his mother stated that she wouldn't be called at work any more to have deal with his behavior. I then explored times when Ray had stood up to Ants' attempts to lure him toward trouble. Ray replied, "Sometimes I just sit there and don't want to play Ants' game." His mother identified several times when Ray had sat still and completed work or done tasks without becoming disruptive. When his teacher was contacted she also provided examples that contradicted the problem story and revealed a valued one.

Over the next few weeks, instances of Ray standing up to Ants were documented. These were shared with other family members and school personnel. During the last quarter of the school year Ray was given a certificate for "debugging himself" from Ants.

Externalization also can be used with groups. For example, if a group of residents has been bickering and arguing with one another, an RYCW could do group externalization as a way of determining how the problem has interfered with the residents' relationships, times when the residents are able to tame bickering, and so on. The same steps would apply, with the only difference being that a group would work on the problem. This is similar to using externalization with families.

Externalizing conversations can help youth and others around them to reauthor stories that run counter to problematic ones. Valued stories can provide youth with a positive sense of self and "being," which is crucial for young people (Bertolino, 1999). It should be noted that sometimes youth have difficulty with externalizing conversations. When this is the case, it's up to the RYCW to find what works and to converse with youth in a way that's right for them.

CREATING COMPELLING FUTURES
WITH POSSIBILITIES

The Moving Walkway: From Problem to Possibility

We've discussed that youth and others often find themselves in corners merely because of the way in which their situations are described or *languaged*. In turn, how RYCWs talk with youth can have a significant influence on the stories that evolve. In Chapter 3, some ways of introducing the element of possibility through dialoguing were offered. We learned how to paint doorways in corners with language and in some way subtly interject possibilities into otherwise closed-down views. Possibility-laced language provides the key for opening up these situations.

Another way to begin to open up possibilities for change through language is by using the "moving walkway" (Bertolino, 1999; O'Hanlon, 1996; O'Hanlon and Bertolino, 1998). Just as airports contain moving conveyor belts that take people to their destinations, our use of language can do the same. Although youth and others may come to us with views and stories without possibilities, there are ways of interviewing, asking questions, making comments, and telling stories that can create an effect similar to that of the moving walkway (O'Hanlon and Bertolino, 1998). That is, by using language as a conveyor belt, we can help youth to create a compelling sense of a future with possibilities before they even take any action. Just as moving walkways transport people toward their destinations with little effort on their part, we can help youth to move toward future possibilities without any conscious effort on their part. The following material presents three particular ways of doing this.

Use Expectancy Talk

Assume the possibility of youth and others finding solutions by using words and phrases such as "yet" and "so far." Such language presupposes that even though things feel stuck or unchangeable in the present, sometime in the future they will change. This simple shift in language can help to create a "light at the end of the tunnel":

Youth: I'll never be any good at anything.

RYCW: So far you haven't attained the level of skill you'd like.

Youth: I'm always in trouble.

RYCW: You haven't found a way to stay out of trouble yet.

Youth: I don't have a future. Why should I even try?

RYCW: Up to this point, you haven't found a reason to try to make things better in your life.

Turn Problems into Goals

Recast the problem statement into a statement about the preferred future or goal:

Youth: I'll never get out of the gang.

RYCW: So you'd like to be able to find a way to get out of the gang?

Youth: No one cares what happens to me.

RYCW: So you'd like to know that people care about you?

Youth: I've been in trouble all of my life.

RYCW: So one of the things that we could do in here is to help you to find a way to change your relationship with trouble?

Use Presupposition

Presuppose that changes and progress toward goals will occur by using words such as "when" and "will."

Youth: No one wants to hang out with me because all I do is get into trouble.

RYCW: So when you start to make friends, how do you think you'll act differently?

Youth: I can't stop. All I know how to do is get in trouble.

RYCW: So when you've put trouble behind you, what will you be doing?

Youth: All people do is blame me.

> **RYCW:** When you're no longer feeling blamed, how will things be different?

By using the moving walkway to introduce possibilities through language, RYCWs can begin to create openings where walls seemed to previously exist. This way of talking with youth is an ongoing process; it is a way that RYCWs can continue to open pathways throughout the course of placement. By using possibility language such as that associated with the moving walkway, we can begin to introduce the idea of change by challenging and casting doubt on attentional patterns and problematic stories.

Cocreating Preferred Futures

Upon entering residential placement, youth often present themselves as having no view or vision of the future. In addition, other mental health professionals, family members, teachers, and juvenile officers will sometimes convey the idea that a youth is incapable of change or, perhaps, has no future. After hearing such a story from a respected professional, it can seem that a youth really is doomed. So, how can RYCWs avoid being induced into accepting these types of stories? One way to do this is to help youth to cocreate a sense of a preferred future, that is, a future in which things work out, a problem is resolved, or a goal is reached.

When thinking of the future, it is common for most RYCWs to think of the past or present as causing the present and the future. In fact, we often live our lives by this adage and say to youth, "That will affect your future." But, what if the future could have an effect on, or even cause, the present or the past? Consider these situations: If you knew that you were going to win the lottery tomorrow would you go to work? If you knew that something bad was going to happen to someone you cared about, would you take action to prevent it? By knowing the future, your actions in the present can be influenced. Thus, we believe that by helping youth to cocreate preferred futures, the present and past can be affected.

Before moving on to ways of cocreating preferred futures, it is important to consider the three things that we have outlined in Table 5.1.

TABLE 5.1. Considerations for Cocreating Preferred Futures with Youth

---

• *Cocreate realistic and attainable futures*—RYCWs must work with youth to establish preferred futures that are possible. That is something that can be attained by youth given who they are, including their situations, resources, and capabilities. Some things are unchangeable, even though they may truly be what a youth wants (e.g., bringing back a deceased parent, never having to do any form of schoolwork, etc.).

• *Cocreate legal and ethical futures*—RYCWs must make sure that preferred futures are within the law and ethical. For example, it is not okay to set a future vision of being a gang member (if the gang is one that is involved in illegal actions). As discussed earlier, some behaviors are okay and others are not. Therapists should support those future visions which are legal, ethical, and promote health and well-being and stand against those which are illegal, unethical, and harmful to self or others.

• *Attention is on small changes*—While long-term or larger future visions may be established, it is important for RYCWs to attend to signs or small changes that may indicate that a youth is heading in the desired direction. As mentioned in Chapter 2, if youth have the feeling that they are moving forward they may feel less frustrated and more hopeful. It is also important that others (i.e., parents, social service workers, etc.) are clear as to what signs may represent movement toward established visions.

The following are a few ways that RYCWs can work with adolescents and families to cocreate preferred futures.

The Crystal Ball

This method is based on a hypnotic technique developed by Milton Erickson (1954). Although Erickson used trance with his crystal ball method, it also can be done nonhypnotically. When Bob uses a variation of this approach, he provides a dry-erase board, an assortment of crayons and markers, and paper for drawing (Bertolino, 1999). He first has the youth draw a picture of three crystal balls, or three "windows," that represent the past, present, and future. Next, the youth draws a picture of himself or herself inside each of the crystal balls or windows. He then asks several questions about the first two pictures that represent the past and present:

- What are you doing in this (past/present) crystal ball/window?
- What are you thinking about in this (past/present) crystal ball/window?
- What are you feeling in this (past/present) crystal ball/window?
- What would you like to have happen in this (past/present) crystal ball/window?

Next, Bob moves on to the drawing that represents the future and says:

> As you look into this crystal ball/window, imagine that you are now in the future and things are going well for you. You're happy that things are better, and people around you seem to be happier too.

This is followed with a few more questions:

- How did things get better?
- Where did your problem go?
- What did you do to help solve the problem?
- What did others do to help solve the problem?
- What did I do to help you solve the problem?
- Who else knows that the problem is gone?
- How do they know?
- What will you do if the problem tries to come back?

We will often hear very interesting and ingenious stories from youth about how their problems were solved. Older youth may be less interested in displaying their artistic talents, so sometimes it may work better for the RYCW to draw three circles on a dry-erase board and proceed from there. The idea is to get a glimpse of what youth's lives will be like when they are no longer being hindered by the problem. Once that becomes clear, steps can be taken to achieve that preferred outcome and future.

Miracle Questions and Beyond

Steve de Shazer (1988) and colleagues at the Brief Family Therapy Center (BFTC) in Milwaukee, Wisconsin, developed the "miracle question" as a way of helping clients to envision their lives when their problem is solved. The original form of the question is as follows:

> Suppose you were to go home tonight, and while you were asleep, a miracle happened and this problem was solved. How will you know the miracle happened? What will be different? (p. 5)

This is a useful question, particularly with adults; however, we have found it to be a bit too difficult for some youth. We prefer a slightly different form (Bertolino, 1999):

> Suppose that when you went home tonight and went to sleep, something strange happened to you and your life changed for the better. You may or may not know what actually happened, but you knew that your problem had gone away. What will be different? (p. 75)

Instead of using the term "miracle," we substitute words such as "strange" or "weird." Some youth won't take well to the idea of miracles happening, while others will readily respond. Words such as strange and weird can be broad for adults but seem to suit youth well. Another idea is to substitute a word that a youth has come up with in the place of miracle, strange, or weird. When using questions of this nature, it is important to find out specifically what the youth will be *doing*. That is, what actions will be happening. The focus on actions moves the discussion into the realm in which he or she has some choices and power to make changes.

Videotape Descriptions

Several previous publications have highlighted the use of videotape descriptions in a variety of situations (Bertolino, 1999; O'Hanlon and Bertolino, 1998; O'Hanlon and Wilk, 1987; Hudson and O'Hanlon, 1991). We have found this idea to be particularly useful with youth in helping them to create futures with possibilities. Again, the idea is to have them describe a time down the road when things are going the way they like. In the recent past, Bill O'Hanlon and Bob Bertolino (1998) offered this example:

> Let's say that a few weeks, months, or time had elapsed and your problem had been resolved. If you and I were to watch a videotape of your life in the future, what would you be doing on that tape that would show that things were better? (p. 90)

This method allows RYCWs to obtain action-oriented descriptions of how things will be when the problem is no longer present. Then, the RYCW can help the youth move toward that preferred reality.

The Time Machine

Another way that is helpful in getting youth to catch a glimpse of their preferred future is to use the "time machine." Selekman (1997) has used this concept to help children propel into the past and the future. We typically use it as a future-based method, as we want youth to get the sense that what they envision in the future can have an effect on what they are currently doing. Here's typically how we tell a youth about the time machine (Bertolino, 1999):

> Let's say there is a time machine sitting here in the office. This time machine can take you wherever you want to go. Now let's say that you climb in and it propels you into the future to a time when things are going the way you want them to go.

We then proceed to ask the youth some of these questions:

- Where are you?
- What is happening?
- How is your life different?
- What can you bring back with you to help you out in the present time?
- How would it help you in the present time?

The RYCW can then work with the youth to apply the vision to the here and now.

FutureWorks

In the classic children's book, *Harold and the Purple Crayon* (Johnson, 1955), one evening, a little boy named Harold decides to go for a walk. All he takes with him is a purple crayon. But with his crayon he is able to construct a wonderful adventure. Just as Harold used a crayon, we can invite youth to construct artistic images of their preferred futures.

This is an extremely flexible idea. Youth can draw, paint, make a collage out of pictures from old magazines, make a board game, or create new ways of constructing their vision of a preferred future. Here's how we typically introduce this idea (Bertolino, 1999):

> With the markers, paper, glue, magazines, and other stuff I have here I'd like you to make something that will show me how you'd like the future to be for you (and your family).

As the "futurework" is being made, the RYCW can ask questions or help out if the youth wants. Once completed, the RYCW can ask about what is happening in the youth's future and what he or she could do now to begin to move in that direction. The RYCW also can ask if he or she can add something to the futurework. If approval is given, then an obstacle, such as a magazine clipping of a liquor bottle or a spelled-out a phrase such as bad grades should be added. Then the youth can be asked how he or she might deal with what has been added. Clippings that represent positive things also can be added.

This particular method can be an ongoing individual or group project in residential treatment. That is, RYCWs can work with youth on their futureworks over longer periods of time, dealing with a variety of concerns that arise. In addition, all of the ideas presented here can be modified and used as group exercises.

Many have discussed the importance of attending to people's preferred views (Eron and Lund, 1996; Rogers, 1961). With youth, this seems especially important, as their stories about themselves seem to play a vital role in overcoming obstacles. In addition, the stories that others have about adolescents can also have tremendous impact. All of the approaches described can help youth to rehabilitate or create a vision of a future with possibilities. We can then work backward from the future to the present to figure out what they can do currently, if indeed that were their future. When youth can envision and gain a sense of a future where things are better, it can be a catalyst for setting things in motion.

Future Pull: Finding a Vision for the Future

The following list of questions can be helpful with youth in creating a better present and preferred future and can assist RYCWs in becoming clear about youth's perspectives and what they want for themselves and, perhaps, others around them (Bertolino, 1999; O'Hanlon and Bertolino, 1998):

- What do you think is important for you to accomplish during your youth/teenage years?
- What is your vision of a good future?
- What dreams did you or do you have for yourself in upcoming days/weeks/months/years and throughout your life?
- What are you here on the planet for?
- What are teenagers/young people/human beings on the planet for, in your view?
- What area do you think you could you make a contribution in?
- What would you try to do with your life if you knew that you could not fail?

Dealing with and Dissolving Barriers to the Preferred Future

Sometimes youth are clear about where they want to go with their lives, but they cannot get there because they perceive insurmountable barriers in their way. They have fears of success or fears of failure. They think they are inadequate to the task of making the dream happen, or they think certain things must happen before they begin to pursue their dreams. Again, here is a list of questions that might prove helpful in clarifying these perceived barriers (Bertolino, 1999; O'Hanlon and Bertolino, 1998):

- What, in your view, stops you from getting to where you want to be with your life?
- What, in your view, stops you from realizing your dreams or getting to your goals?

- What do you believe must happen before you can realize your dreams/future?
- What are the actions you haven't taken to make your dreams and visions come true?
- What things stand in your way of realizing your dreams and visions?
- What would your heroes, models, or people you admire do if they were you to make this dream or vision happen?
- What are you not doing, feeling, or thinking that they would in this situation?
- What are you doing, feeling, or thinking that they wouldn't?

Making an Action Plan to Reach the Preferred Future

Having a vision of the future, and even realizing what the perceived barriers are, will not necessarily take youth to that future. There must be a plan of action and a way to start to take some of those actions to make the future happen. Here are some ideas and questions that can help youth to formulate and put into practice actions that will likely create their preferred futures:

- What could you do in the near future that would be steps toward getting you to where you want to be?
- What could you do in the near future that would be steps toward realizing your visions and dreams?
- What would be a first step toward realizing your dream/ future?
- What will you do as soon as you leave here?
- What will you do tonight?
- What will you be thinking that would help you take those steps?

With most youth who are stuck in their troubles, just getting them to turn their gaze from the past to the future is a major reorientation. This reorientation can provide information about directions for treatment, as well as meaning and purpose in their lives, and lead to the restoration of hope.

In the next chapter, we'll offer ideas about how RYCWs can help youth to change unhelpful patterns of action, interaction, and context.

Chapter 6

Pete and Repeat:
Altering Problematic Patterns
of Action, Interaction, and Context

Fall seven times, stand up eight.

Japanese Proverb

PROBLEMATIC PATTERNS OF ACTION
AND INTERACTION

Just as the views that youth and others hold can be problematic, the actions they *do* can be troublesome. When problematic patterns are repeated, it can seem to youth and others as if they're frozen in time or stuck in a time warp without a way of escaping. This chapter will introduce ways that RYCWs can help to change and disrupt problematic patterns and interactions and shift problematic aspects associated with context.

Milton Erickson (Rossi, 1980; Rossi, Ryan, and Sharp, 1983) was fascinated with how people *did* their problems. In fact, he frequently mapped out the details of his patients' problems. Erickson would focus on the problem at hand so intently that it was as if he were studying the person to play him or her in a movie. Similarly, Neurolinguistic Programming (NLP) cocreator Richard Bandler, who along with John Grinder (Bandler and Grinder, 1975; Grinder, DeLozier, and Bandler, 1977) meticulously studied Erickson's work, often has asked clients, "If I were you, how would I do your problem?" Essentially, both Erickson and Bandler demonstrated the importance of learning the patterns that people do on a personal basis.

We view this position of curiosity as important for RYCWs. Youth regularly repeat patterns that continue to keep them stuck. Similarly, RYCWs may repeat actions and interactions that only serve to keep the problematic pattern going. However, by using creativity and by studying problematic patterns, RYCWs can learn new ways of intervening and of ultimately using what works.

In a past publication, Bill O'Hanlon and Bob Bertolino (1998) discussed identifying problematic patterns:

> We explore with clients the negative problem patterns that seem to be inhibiting or intruding in their lives. We seek to be geographers, exploring the topography and coastline of Problem-Land. We want to know the details of the problem or symptom, and help the client to find ways of escaping it. (p. 66)

By isolating the problem, the RYCW can intervene in the patterns that make up the problem or change the contexts around it so they no longer contain the problem or symptom (Bertolino, 1999; O'Hanlon, 1982, 1987; O'Hanlon and Bertolino, 1998; O'Hanlon and Wilk, 1987; O'Hanlon and Weiner-Davis, 1989).

Youth and others' descriptions of problems help us to understand what they mean by the words they use, so our own interpretations aren't imposed as much on their words. We're also searching for any aspect of a problem that repeats. This indicates a pattern. What we want to do is explore aspects of the problem pattern. To ferret out the patterns of the problem, RYCWs want to find out the following:

- How often does the problem typically happen (once an hour, once a day, once a week)?
- What is the typical timing (time of day, time of week, time of month, time of year) of the problem?
- What is the duration of the problem (how long it typically lasts)?
- Where does the problem typically happen (spatial patterns)?
- What does the person and others who are around usually do when the problem is happening?

Once a problematic pattern is identified, RYCWs can begin to help youth to change the doing of the problem.

CHANGING THE DOING OF PROBLEMATIC PATTERNS OF ACTION AND INTERACTION

RYCWs can help to alter or change problematic patterns of action and interaction in two ways:

1. Alter the repetitive pattern of action or interaction involved in the problem.
2. Identify and encourage the use of solution patterns of action and interaction.

Altering Repetitive Patterns of Action and Interaction Involved in the Problem

The first way to change the doing of the problem is to interrupt or disrupt repetitive patterns involved in or surrounding the problem. Once an RYCW has gathered information about the aspects of the problematic pattern, several methods can be used to interrupt or disrupt the typical pattern of action or interaction. The following are some possibilities.

Change the Duration of the Problem or the Pattern Around the Problem

> An eleven-year-old boy would refuse to go to bed at "lights out." This would usually begin at bedtime and continue for about ten to fifteen minutes. An RYCW told the youth, "I think you ought to refuse to go to bed for longer than just ten or fifteen minutes. From now on, I want you to refuse for at least twenty minutes." The boy was confused by this. The first night when the youth began to wind down before twenty minutes were up, the RYCW told him that he needed to continue. After two evenings, the boy went to bed right away.

Change the Time (Time of Day, Week, Month, or Year)
of the Problem or the Pattern Around the Problem

A fourteen-year-old girl would throw temper tantrums on days when a recreational activity was chosen that she didn't like. The RYCWs noticed that the tantrums were generally at the same time—between 3:00 p.m. and 3:30 p.m. because that's when the residents were told of the afternoon activity. The RYCWs decided to tell the girl of the activity at 2:45 p.m. and inform her that she should have plenty of time to have her tantrum.

Change the Sequence (Order) of Events
Involved in or Around the Problem

A twelve-year-old would return to the residential facility from the off-site school each day and say, "I'm not doing my chores!" She would then refuse for several hours. During a staffing, an RYCW suggested that on the next shift one of the RYCWs meet the girl as soon as she entered the facility after school and emphatically inquire, "Do you want to refuse now or in a few minutes?"

Interrupt or Otherwise Prevent the Occurrence of the Problem

A group of three youth would routinely create disturbances at bedtime and refuse to quiet down. One evening, an RYCW on duty told the three boys, "Since the three of you seem to be so alert at bedtime, I'm going to give you the opportunity to use that alertness." He then brought the three boys into the kitchen on the unit and began to read to them from the daily newspaper. When the boys would begin to doze off, the RYCW would raise his voice and show verbal exuberance in regard to the story being read.

Add a New Element to the Problem

An eleven-year-old boy would frequently walk around the residential facility yelling expletives and then deny the action later. It was decided during a staff meeting that the RYCWs on shift would each carry small, pocket-size, handheld audiotape players and turn them on when the boy began his verbal escapades. The boy was informed of the plan, but the recorders were not needed, as he abandoned the behavior.

Break Up Any Previously Whole Element of the Problem into Smaller Elements

During residential community meetings, two particularly competitive youth would frequently square off and argue with each other. Since these arguments tended to disrupt the groups, an RYCW suggested that the cooking timer from the kitchen be brought in, set for two minutes, and then each boy would have two minutes to offer his point of view. Once the timer went off, it was the other person's turn. They were told to argue one point at a time. When that was resolved, they could move on to the next concern.

Reverse the Direction of Striving in the Performance of the Problem (Paradox)

A young boy in a residential program would throw temper tantrums on a daily basis. This would include screaming and crying. The RYCWs decided to cheerlead and encourage the boy to improve upon previous tantrums. The boy became frustrated and gave up the tantrums.

Link the Occurrence of the Problem to Another Pattern That Is a Burdensome Activity (Ordeal)

A fourteen-year-old boy refused to do his chores. It was decided that whenever this happened, all of the males on his unit would be brought downstairs to do "superchores" (intensive chores).

A collaborative, competency-based approach does not view the RYCW as an expert who knows the answers. Instead, the RYCW works to find out what will change the problematic action or inter-actions of youth. If one idea doesn't work, another is tried.

Tapping into Creativity

There is a saying in the business world that has taken hold lately: "Out of the box thinking." An "in the box, out of the box" metaphor can also be helpful in residential treatment. We encourage RYCWs to be very creative in trying to disrupt and change unwanted pat-terns of behavior. The following story illustrates how creativity can make a difference in changing unwanted behavior:

> A retired man bought a new home near a junior high school. The first few weeks following his move brought peace and contentment. Then the new school year began. The afternoon of the first day of school, three boys came walking down the street, beating on every trash can they encountered. This con-tinued each day until the man decided to take action.
>
> One afternoon, the man walked out and met the young percussionists and said, "You kids are a lot of fun. I like to see you express your exuberance like that. Used to do the same thing when I was your age. I'll give you each a dollar if you promise to come around everyday and do your thing." The boys were elated and agreed to continue their drumming. After a few days, the man approached the boys, and with a sad smile said, "The recession's really putting a big dent in my income. From now on, I'll only be able to pay you fifty cents to beat the cans." Although the boys were displeased, they agreed to continue their banging.
>
> A few days later, the retiree again approached the boys and said, "I haven't received my Social Security check yet, so I'm not going to be able to give you more than twenty-five cents. Will that be okay?" "A lousy quarter!" the drum leader ex-claimed. "If you think we're going to waste our time beating these cans for a quarter, you're nuts! No way, mister. We quit!" The man went on to enjoy peace once again. *(Gentle Spaces News,* 1995, pp. 297-298)

Creativity, spontaneity, and humor can inject a new element into situations involving repetition of annoying patterns. In addition, being creative can allow RYCWs to employ ideas that may have been helpful in other contexts.

Identifying and Encouraging Solution Patterns of Action and Interaction

A second way of changing the doing of problems is for RYCWs to elicit, evoke, and highlight previous solution patterns, abilities, competencies, strengths, and resources (Bertolino, 1999; O'Hanlon, 1998). This does not mean trying to convince youth of their competencies and abilities. For example, an RYCW wouldn't say, "You can do it. Just look at all your strengths!" This can be very invalidating to youth who are stuck. Instead, we might say, "How were you able to do that?" or "What is it about you that you were able to _____?"

We want to continue to acknowledge what is being experienced internally and begin to investigate, as would Sherlock Holmes or Columbo, the wealth of experience and expertise of youth. Through our questions, we work to evoke some sense of competence and experience of solving problems that youth already possess. Sometimes youth get caught up in problematic patterns and have difficulty recalling the experience they have within. The following are four specific ways of encouraging the use of solution patterns of action and interaction.

Find Out About Previous Solutions to the Problem, Including Partial Solutions and Partial Successes

Even in cases where youth appear to be stuck, there are times when they haven't experienced the problem full force or expected to experience the problem but it did not happen. What we want to do is inquire about exceptions to the problem pattern, including past solutions and partial solutions and successes. Here are some possible questions that can help RYCWs to find out about the previous solution attempts of youth:

- Tell me about a time when things didn't go the way you wanted and you got upset, yet you were able to get somewhat

of a handle on the situation. What was different about that
time?

- You've misbehaved five out of the past seven nights. How did
  you keep yourself from misbehaving on the other two nights?
- You mentioned that you usually lose your temper and scream
  when you get mad, but you didn't do that last night. How did
  you do that?
- Tell me about a time when you didn't want to do your chores
  but you decided to anyway. How did you make that decision?

Once again, we are aiming for action descriptions of what youth
are doing or have done differently. We are also *presupposing* that
there have been times when things were better (O'Hanlon and
Weiner-Davis, 1989). We are not asking *if* there have been times.
We are asking what happened, when it happened, and how it happened.

Let's take the example of the youth who typically screams when
he loses his temper and is angry. Here's how an RYCW might
converse with him to evoke a solution pattern:

RYCW: On some previous occasions you've lost your temper
and screamed when you've been angry, but you didn't last
night. How did you do that?

Youth: I just did.

RYCW: What is it that you did differently than the other times
when you've been upset?

Youth: I just told myself "no."

RYCW: Okay. You told yourself "no," and then what happened?

Youth: I just calmed down.

RYCW: Right, and that was different because usually you
would have screamed. Then how did you actually calm down?

Youth: I just told myself, "Don't get in trouble." Then I went
and watched TV.

Sometimes youth will have a hard time relating what they did
differently. In these instances, we can offer multiple-choice options.

With the same example, we might say, "So did you find yourself being quieter than usual, or did you leave the room, or was it something else?" Multiple-choice inquisitions will often lead to clarification on the part of the youth, as he or she will either choose one of the choices or respond, "No, what I actually did was _____."

For many youth, it will be too much to ask, "Tell me about a time when you didn't have the problem." Typical responses to such a question include, "I always have the problem" or "Things are always this way." Thus, as discussed previously in regard to scaling and percentage questions, it is usually better to inquire about small indicators of success or solution patterns. For example, an RYCW might ask, "Tell me about a time when things went a little bit better." Smaller increments of difference will usually be easier for youth to identify.

Should a youth still respond that the problem is never any better, we want to do two things. First, we want to make sure we are acknowledging and validating what the youth is experiencing internally. Then, we can work backward from worst to best. Here's an example of how to do this:

RYCW: You mentioned that you argue a lot with your mom on the phone. Tell me about a time recently when you seemed to argue a bit less.

Youth: Never. We always argue when we talk on the phone.

RYCW: Okay. So it seems to you that in the past when you've talked with your mom on the phone you've argued. And you've already told me that you talk with her daily. So which day this week was the worst?

Youth: Oh, that's easy. It was Friday.

RYCW: What happened?

Youth: She really screamed at me—for nothing.

RYCW: I'm sorry that that happened to you. That must have been tough.

Youth: A little. I'm used to it.

RYCW: Well, if Friday was the worst in recent days, what were Wednesday or Thursday like because they weren't quite as bad as Friday?

Youth: She still yelled, but not as much.

RYCW: What do you think that was all about?

Youth: I think it was because we talked before she started drinking.

We want to acknowledge and validate the experiences of youth, while simultaneously evoking their competencies, abilities, and previous solution attempts in relation to the problem. Generally speaking, it's helpful to use "solution talk" instead of "problem talk." For instance, if an RYCW was using problem talk, he or she might ask, "Tell me about a time when the problem wasn't quite as bad." An example of solution talk might be "Tell me about a time when things were a bit more manageable for you." The idea here is that solution talk can orient adolescents and others toward what's working, as opposed to drawing attention to what is not. However, as illustrated earlier, RYCWs will sometimes need to adjust because a client does not relate to such a focus. RYCWs can do just as well at eliciting and evoking solution patterns by talking about the problem.

Find Out What Happens When the Problem Ends
or Starts to End

The problems that youth have experienced have end points. That is, they always come to an end, if only for a short while. Sometimes solution patterns exist within these times. We want to know how the problem typically ends. We can also ask for more details about aspects of the ending process. Here are some possible questions:

- How do you know when the problem is coming to an end? What's the first thing that you notice?
- How can others tell when the problem has subsided or started to subside?
- What do others do that helps to bring the problem to an end?
- What have you noticed helps you to wind down?

The following case example illustrates how a solution pattern can be found by inquiring about how a problem ends:

> Aaron was verbally teasing and picking on his younger brother "relentlessly" according to his parents. They reported that they were frustrated because they felt their efforts to stop him were futile. The mother remarked, "I know older brothers sometimes tease younger ones but he's really mean and merciless." Aaron was asked, "You've got your parents telling you to knock it off, and you know it's not a cool thing to do, but how do you know when enough is enough and finally get a grip and stop teasing your brother?" Aaron replied, "When my mom tells me I'm gonna be grounded I stop, but she doesn't usually do that until she's tried everything else." (Bertolino, 1999)

By finding out how a problem ends or starts to end, we can also find out how a process might be altered or interrupted. Youth can learn choice points where they can intervene with solution patterns instead of continuing the problem pattern or allowing it to evolve.

Search for Contexts in Which the Youth Feels Competent and Has Good Problem-Solving or Creative Skills

Even though youth may be experiencing problems in specific areas of their lives, oftentimes they have competencies, abilities, or solution patterns in other areas that can be helpful in solving the problem at hand. We want to explore any areas of the youth's lives that they feel good about. This can include jobs, hobbies, sports, clubs, or areas of special knowledge or skill that they have that can be tapped into to solve the problem.

We want to find out about exceptions to the problem. Sometimes referring back to the initial interview can be helpful here, as information about school, social relationships, and contexts in which competency and ability exist have been highlighted. Here's how one might explore various contexts with a youth who is struggling with fighting:

RYCW: So things haven't been going that great here.

Youth: If they'd just get off my case about the fights, everything would be fine.

RYCW: It seems to you as if they're on your case a lot of the time because they're worried about you getting into fights.

Youth: Well, yeah. If people wouldn't say crap to me, I wouldn't be fighting.

RYCW: I can see how that might get to you. I'm curious though, I haven't heard anyone say that you've been fighting at school.

Youth: So?

RYCW: How have you managed to stay on the up-and-up at school?

Youth: I just ignore it and get down to business.

RYCW: How do you do that?

Youth: I stay focused because I want to make it into technical school.

RYCW: So staying focused on your goal of technical school helps you?

Youth: Yep.

RYCW: How can what you do at school be helpful to you on the unit?

Youth: I guess I just need to realize what my goal is.

When we can elicit and evoke abilities, strengths, resources, and solution areas in other parts of a youth's life, we can link them to the problematic area. In addition, we can find times when the problem doesn't occur or happens to a lesser degree. We want to explore these other areas and find out how they can be useful in solving the current problem.

Find Out Why the Problem Isn't Worse

Sometimes it can be helpful to ask why the problem isn't worse. This can do at least two things. First, it can normalize things for youth when they realize that some people do experience worse situations. Second, it can yield information about what they've done to keep things from deteriorating further. Questions commonly used here are sometimes referred to as coping-sequence questions (Berg and Gallagher, 1991; Selekman, 1993, 1997). Here are some examples:

- Why aren't things worse with your situation?
- What have you done to keep things from getting worse?
- What steps have you taken to prevent things from heading downhill any further?
- What else has helped keep things from becoming worse?
- How has that made a difference with your situation?

The following case example illustrates the use of coping sequence questions:

> Anita had been failing some of her classes in the public school program she was attending through her residential facility. One evening, a curious RYCW asked, "How come you haven't failed all of your classes?" She responded, "Some of my classes are easy." The RYCW then asked, "Yeah, but you still could have not done anything at all and bottomed out. What did you do to keep things from getting worse?" To this, Anita replied, "I did my work in class." The RYCW went on to explore Anita's method of not bottoming out and was able to help her apply this method to her other classes.

When youth are asked why things aren't worse, they're often caught off guard. Such a focus orients youth to what they've done that has helped to keep the problem at bay. Sometimes this can help to build some sense of hope in those cases where youth feel that nothing is going right.

CHANGING THE CONTEXT

Contextual elements are those aspects of a youth's world that surround the problem but aren't necessarily directly involved in the problem (O'Hanlon and Bertolino, 1998; O'Hanlon and O'Hanlon, 1999). Aspects of context come in two varieties. The first involves time and spatial patterns. Time patterns include when, how frequently, and how long the problem happens. Spatial patterns have to do with where the problem typically happens. Both time and spatial patterns were discussed earlier in this chapter. This section will focus on the second variety, aspects of context.

The second variety involves cultural background, family and historical background, biochemical/genetic background, gender training, and any propensities associated with these aspects. As RYCWs, we want to explore the patterns that come from these aspects and consider their influence in supporting the problem. It is important that RYCWs are careful not to imply that influencing factors are *causing* the problem. As discussed in regard to resiliency, each youth is unique and should be treated as such. Thus, just because a youth comes from a family that has a history of alcoholism does not mean that he or she will become alcoholic. Also, having a genetic or biochemical propensity for depression does not necessarily make one depressed. As with the viewing and the doing of problems, we want to explore problematic aspects and patterns of contextual influence and solution aspects of the context:

> Bob worked with a fifteen-year-old male who was referred for counseling due to being violent toward his mother and classmates. He also had an older and younger brother who had experienced similar difficulties. When the problem was explored, he found that the father had been a violent man, as had his father. Bob asked a few questions such as, "How did you learn about how men should act in your family?" and, "Where did you get the idea that violence was an appropriate way of dealing with things?" He then explored solution patterns: "Who in your family has not bought into the idea that violence is the way to handle things?" "What are some other ways that the men in your family have dealt with problems?" (Bertolino, 1999)

In every problem involving a contextual element, there are problematic influences as well as solution patterns and competencies.

We want to search for the exceptions and solution patterns that run counter to the problematic patterns.

Context can be used to normalize and highlight strengths. If a youth begins to understand that given the context in which the problem occurred, many people would experience, think, feel, or do something similar, it often lessens shame and the feelings of isolation (O'Hanlon and O'Hanlon, 1999). For example, with the case just discussed, the fifteen-year-old was complimented for standing opposed to the idea in his family that "Men are tough and should do whatever it takes to get control." Aspects of context can either be problematic or helpful. We want to highlight those which promote problem resolution while simultaneously holding youth accountable.

IDENTIFYING AND AMPLIFYING CHANGE

As we work to change aspects of viewing, actions, and context with youth, we want to continually search for exceptions to troublesome behavior and indicators that change is occurring in a preferred direction. To do this, RYCWs identify and amplify change. First we work to *identify* change by watching for those small signs that have been discussed in staffings or that a youth has identified. Let's refer to a case example that illustrates this point:

> In staffing, the treatment team established a goal for a resident, Robbie. The goal was that Robbie would talk out problems with other residents without hitting them when he became angry. It was agreed that one sign that Robbie was making progress toward this goal would be when he started to get angry but did not escalate to hitting another resident. Another would be when he listened to staff and backed away from a resident when he was becoming agitated and upset. Staff members were directed to watch for moments when these and other possible signs of change were occurring.
>
> During the first week following the team meeting, an RYCW observed Robbie in a dispute with another male resident. When the RYCW felt that the situation might escalate further, she asked Robbie to step away. After a slight hesitation, he did so.

The stepping away action was an indication that Robbie might be changing his previous pattern of hitting others when he becomes angry. Of course, one incident may not indicate a change in a pattern. The importance of identifying the exception to the problem behavior is twofold. First, it demonstrates to youth and others that there are alternative behaviors that can be used. Second, by identifying alternative actions to the problematic ones, RYCWs can have conversations with youth about what they did differently. This can help to empower youth. Let's see how Robbie's actions were identified by the RYCW on shift:

> **RYCW:** Robbie, that was great that you were able to back off when things were getting heated. Nice going, I'm proud of you. Did you notice that?
>
> **Robbie:** Yeah.

Once we've identified a sign or signs of change, we want to *amplify* any change. Here's one way of doing this:

> **RYCW:** So tell me, how did you do what you did?
>
> **Robbie:** I don't know.
>
> **RYCW:** You know, there have been times that you haven't responded as well to staff when they've asked you to step back. But this time, you seemed to do something different. Any idea what that might have been?
>
> **Robbie:** I know I don't want to be in trouble.
>
> **RYCW:** Okay. So you don't want to be in trouble. Anything else?
>
> **Robbie:** Not really.
>
> **RYCW:** How often do you think you catch yourself and stop yourself from doing things that you get in trouble for?
>
> **Robbie:** I do it all the time, but you don't see it.
>
> **RYCW:** Really? You know I thought that about you. I was thinking that maybe you were able to get the upper hand with your anger more often than you've shown around staff.

Robbie: Yeah.

RYCW: So I'm curious, what needs to happen so that you can continue to tame your anger and not let it push you around?

Robbie: I just need to keep backing off.

RYCW: What can we do to help you?

Robbie: Just signal me when you see me getting mad.

RYCW: How should we signal you?

Robbie: Just say, "Robbie, time-out," and give a time-out signal.

RYCW: We can do that. What can you do if we're not around?

Robbie: I'll just tell myself to not get in trouble.

RYCW: And that will signal you?

Robbie: Yep.

RYCW: And then what will you do?

Robbie: I'll step back.

The change is amplified by the RYCW continuing to discuss what the youth did, how he or she did it, and what it will take for him or her to do it more often in the future. In addition, the RYCW can inquire as to how others might be of assistance in helping the youth to continue his or her new or desired actions. The importance of this process cannot be overstated. Often youth do not recognize those moments, however small or short, when they have influence over the problem. When RYCWs call attention to those small indicators of change and then move to amplify them, youth can become aware of what *specific* things they may be doing that made a difference in the present and may be of help in contending with future problems.

Using Speculation

Frequently, when positive change has occurred, youth will have few ideas about what contributed to the change. Here's an example of what we're talking about:

> **RYCW:** How did you manage to complete four out of the five assignments you were given?
>
> **Youth:** I don't know.
>
> **RYCW:** What did you do differently than before?
>
> **Youth:** Nothing.

When youth respond in ways similar to this example, it's important that RYCWs do not minimize the significance of such interactions. Throughout this book, we have discussed the importance of any interactions with youth. Thus, the mere fact that an RYCW is highlighting desired actions will offer a youth a different perspective on a problem.

Another possibility can be helpful with youth in residential placement. Bob (Bertolino, 1999) has written about the use of *speculation* in amplifying change. This is a simple process that also can work to empower youth. The idea is for an RYCW to offer up possible interpretations about what may be contributing to the change. The key is that these interpretations are the types of things that youth are unlikely to reject. These include, but are not limited to, such things as "age, maturity, becoming wiser, and thinking more of other people's feelings" (Bertolino, 1999, p. 144). Using the case example given a moment ago, here's how to do this:

> **RYCW:** So you're not sure what you did differently to complete most of your assignments?
>
> **Youth:** No.
>
> **RYCW:** You know, I wonder if part of it is because you're growing up and you want to leave behind some of the younger behaviors you used to do that don't help you anymore. Maybe you're getting a new view of things and are becoming more mature. I don't know. That's just what I was thinking about you.

The idea is to offer some possibilities that may help to solidify identified change. To do this, we use a position of *conjecture*. We do not attempt to establish truths about the reasons for a youth's behavior. What we do is *offer* some possibilities. Ultimately, youth will accept or reject our offerings based on what they feel is accurate for them.

In our experience, most youth will not totally reject speculations given by RYCWs. They will not say, "I'm not getting more mature!" In fact, when we use this process, we typically see youth perk up and smile. Our experience is that most youth want to be seen as wiser, smarter, more mature, and so forth. In retrospect, for youth to live up to the description that is offered by the RYCW, they must continue to act mature, and so on, therefore leaving little room for the problematic behavior.

Speculation also can be used as an adjunct when a youth has identified what he or she has done differently (Bertolino, 1999). For example, if a youth says, "I told him I didn't want to fight anymore," an RYCW might add, "That's great. I wonder if that's in any way related to your becoming a more a mature person and getting wiser." Again, these types of small interchanges between RYCWs and youth can help youth to become empowered and to develop an improved sense of self.

Move to an Experiential Level

The idea that RYCWs and clinicians alike must get to the "root" feelings for "real" change to occur is a philosophy held by many. We hold a different view. In fact, for most of the youth with whom we've worked, a change in feelings has not led to changes in their lives. We believe that when youth arrive at a different sense of themselves through new views, actions, or interactions, associated feelings will change. Durrant (1993) stated:

> The question becomes not one of "Do we take feelings into account?" but rather "How do we take them into account?" My belief is that acknowledgment of feelings is crucial but not in itself what brings about change. Feelings are one manifestation of a person's constructs or view of self. That is, how I feel in a particular situation will depend upon how I make sense of myself and the situation. Thus, a change in feelings requires a change in constructs in the same way as does a change in behavior." (p. 187)

We have stressed that it is important to acknowledge and validate what youth experience internally, yet we do not focus much on drawing out the feelings of youth and attending to affective experience through questioning. Regardless, we regularly hear about feelings and experiences and attend to them in our work with youth in residential treatment. Ironically, much of our work is extremely cathartic, even though we ask few "feeling" questions. The fact is this: RYCWs do not have to ask feeling-oriented questions to find out about feelings. Since many youth in residential placements are "treatment wise," they are used to hearing the proverbial question "How does that make you feel?" Thus, we don't automatically go for such contrived forms of questioning because they usually produce contrived answers.

We move to an experiential level in a different way. We don't start with experientially based questions, but we use them as a means of solidifying and "anchoring" change. To do this, we identify and amplify change and then ask the youth how he or she experienced the change:

- What was that like for you that you were able to stop yourself and not fight?
- How did that feel when you recognized that it was you who took control?

We also will ask how the youth experienced the by-products of the change:

- What's that like for you knowing that Ms. Richards has noticed that you're changing?
- It seems that a lot of people have really changed their minds about you. What does that feel like knowing that that's happening?

These types of questions can help RYCWs to work with youth to "tap into themselves" experientially, without having to do so in a formulaic way. In this way, feelings are explored, but the process is not considered absolutely necessary for change to occur.

In the next chapter, we'll explore the concept of accountability and ways that RYCWs can work to promote it within residential placements.

Chapter 7

"Houston, We Have a Problem": Managing Crisis with an Eye on Possibilities

The one unchangeable certainty is that nothing is unchangeable or certain.

John F. Kennedy

In residential facilities, the only truly predictable thing is that things are unpredictable. Anything can happen at any time. Therefore, RYCWs must be prepared for a variety of situations and occurrences. Oftentimes, this translates directly to managing crises that seem to emerge "out of nowhere." The RYCW's job becomes one of ensuring the safety of each of the residents and ultimately "holding down the fort."

CRISIS

But what exactly is crisis? Broadly, it's when a person becomes so upset or angry that he or she is a clear threat to his or her own safety or the safety of other people (Crone, 1984). In residential treatment facilities, due to the nature of the populations served, crisis can arise at any moment. On any given day, RYCWs may manage multiple crises or potential crisis situations. Common occurrences that can constitute crisis in residential facilities include self-destructive or self-harming behavior (including self-mutilation), running away, suicidal gestures, verbal escalation, physical aggression, fights between youth, stealing or being stolen from, refusal to comply with rules, and drug or alcohol use. There also are a myriad of other types of crisis situations—some small, some large, but all relative. Crisis is crisis.

Most facilities regularly train RYCWs in crisis intervention approaches. Beyond this, agencies typically have policies and procedures in place that RYCWs are expected to follow in dealing with incidents of crisis. We encourage RYCWs to follow the particular rules of protocol designated by their respective agencies. What we offer here are some ideas that we believe serve as an adjunct to preestablished training and agency policies and procedures regarding crisis management.

The Rule Above All Others: Safety First

The primary responsibility of RYCWs in crisis situations is to ensure the safety of all residents and staff (Durrant, 1993). In times of crisis, training and common sense are perhaps the best assets that RYCWs can possess. Although most problems are not resolved in the heat of crisis, if an RYCW can help to decrease the anxiety of a situation and create a calmer climate, then the likelihood that resolution can be gained is greatly increased.

In times of crisis, we generally find it best to move other residents and staff away from the situation and give the particular youth who is having trouble time to cool down. When there is more than one youth involved, again, we typically want to separate them. This not only ensures safety but it also gives staff time to assess the situation. We also find it important not to be overly concerned with consequences during crisis situations. The determination and delivery of consequences, if necessary, can wait until a later time when things are calmer and more manageable.

Consulting with Co-Workers

In the event of crisis, it's a good idea to collaborate with co-workers. Oftentimes, a staff member has a particularly strong therapeutic relationship with the distressed youth or has done something that worked to de-escalate him or her previously. Therefore, in times of crisis, it can be especially helpful to tap into the expertise of co-workers. Sometimes, bringing in the varying perspectives of our co-workers can help to open possibilities and help RYCWs to view a situation differently.

Paying Attention to Nonverbals

In the heat of crisis, youth may not hear the voices of RYCWs. Still, they are likely to take note of the posture of RYCWs. An awareness of body language can make a difference. We want to avoid clenched fists, crossed arms, hands on hips, and other gestures that could convey hostility, superiority, passing judgment, or an unwillingness to listen to youth's stories. There's also awareness of personal space. That is, we do not want to be "in the face" of youth. We can maintain an appropriate distance that will give youth space and simultaneously make it easy for RYCWS to further intervene, if necessary.

Acknowledgment and Validation Revisited

When RYCWs are working one on one with youth in an effort to de-escalate crises, there are many possibilities. What we want to convey is our unwavering belief that youth can make good present and future choices despite what may have transpired in the past. To do this, we want to always remember to first acknowledge whatever a youth is feeling and experiencing internally. Simply helping youth to feel heard and understood can help to diffuse many crises. Here's an example:

> Kevin was in the clinical office of one of the facilities for which he worked when he noticed a youth whom he had worked with in the past. The youth was refusing to attend a problem-solving group with his housemates and had walked outside. Two staff members, on separate occasions, went out to the porch and insisted that the youth attend the meeting or there would be consequences. Both times, the youth refused and became belligerent.
>
> Kevin approached the youth and asked him what was going on. The youth told about how he was pissed at his housemates and how he felt hurt and targeted by others. He stated that going to the meeting would only make things worse. Kevin allowed the youth to say what he had to say, initially speaking only when acknowledging and validating his feelings. The two then discussed possible options and what the possible conse-

quences might be regarding each decision. Kevin then inquired as to what the youth wanted to do. The boy decided to return to the meeting.

There also is talk we ought to avoid. For example, we want to avoid giving directives. Many youth are used to being given orders from staff. As mentioned, discussion of consequences also can wait until a later time. Further, we want to avoid premature interpretations and conversations that search for the root of a problem. Interpretations can feel like put-downs and may contribute to defensiveness or escalation. Instead, we focus on conversations that help youth to feel heard, understood, and capable of making good choices, even though they may be in a difficult situation. Youth who are talking are not acting, so encouraging them to tell their stories is important.

De-Escalating Crisis Through Exception Searching

In Chapter 6, we discussed that all problems come to an end, and this can provide an excellent opportunity to search for exceptions and solutions. We can move to punctuate the *ending* of a crisis through exception searching. In the midst of crisis, we can search for exceptions and suggest to youth that they have within their experience the ability to respond positively and bring a crisis to an end. That is, RYCWs can suggest to youth that they have choice and influence over the problem. Here's one way of doing this:

> **Youth:** He better back off or I'm gonna pop him!
>
> **RYCW:** I can see you're mad, Gary, and you have a right to be. And though you're mad, I've seen you make some great decisions lately, so I'm wondering if you can use that expertise you've built up to make another.

Here's another possibility with the same case:

> **RYCW:** Gary, you've told me about how when you were in school and you became angry, you were able to calm yourself down by taking deep breaths. I wonder if you can begin to do that now.

We are not trying to speak positive to youth and say, "You can do it!" Our aim is to orient youth to the abilities that they have spoken about or that others have observed.

After the Fire: Building the Muscles of Youth

Once a crisis has been resolved, at some point in the future, it's important that an RYCW or other staff member talk with the youth involved to see how he or she can use the crisis experience to build his or her (*fill in the blank*) muscle. That is, how can the youth use his or her muscle (e.g., good decision making, calming down, etc.) that helped him or her in this crisis in future situations? Here's one way of doing this:

> **RYCW:** You were really able to use your "calming-down muscle" yesterday when Samantha called you a name. How did you do that?
>
> **Youth:** She always does that stuff.
>
> **RYCW:** Yeah, but this time you didn't respond to her as you have in the past.
>
> **Youth:** I know. I stopped myself quicker.
>
> **RYCW:** That's right. How did you flex that muscle just at the right time?
>
> **Youth:** I just told myself that she doesn't matter because all she wants to do is get me in trouble.

We want to amplify those moments of exception and alternative actions that signify change. We believe that this can empower youth to think and act differently in future situations involving conflict or decision making. Here's another possibility:

> **RYCW:** Matt, as pissed off as you were, how did you get yourself to pull back from hitting Jason?
>
> **Youth:** I just did.
>
> **RYCW:** That was impressive. You could have gone on and made the situation worse, but somehow you were able to get

the upper hand with yourself. It's like you used your "pull-back muscles."

Youth: Yeah. I think I did.

We have discussed that it is not necessary for youth to always know what they did differently. In fact, the norm is more that they will not know. However, through the RYCW identifying and amplifying an exception, the youth is offered a different view. Such views can demonstrate to youth their influence over the problem.

A third approach is for RYCWs to use their own observations that have collected over time to help a youth recognize his or her influence over a problem and build preventive muscles. Here's an example:

RYCW: You know, you were able to calm yourself down more quickly this time than you have done in the past. How were you able to do that?

Youth: I guess I just knew I had to. I don't know.

RYCW: It seems that you're quicker at it than you thought.

Youth: I can be quick.

All of the ideas offered here serve to evoke and elicit the strengths and abilities of youth as a way of promoting resilience against the adversities they face. This, we believe, can prevent, or at least decrease, incidents of crisis.

Crisis Debriefing: Finding What Worked

We've found it helpful, following a crisis, for those staff involved to get together and explore the dynamics surrounding the incident. Table 7.1 offers some possible questions for RYCWs to use during these "debriefing sessions."

It is important to remain flexible. If something isn't working, try something else. In doing this, RYCWs should remember to respond to the individual youth, not to the expectations of a particular theory. By maintaining a belief in change and avoiding pathology-based language and unhelpful assumptions, pathways with possibilities can be explored.

TABLE 7.1. Questions for Use During Postcrisis Debriefing

POSTCRISIS DEBRIEFING FOR RYCWS
1. How was the safety of the youth and staff ensured?
2. Is there anything that should be done differently in regard to safety?
3. Was there time for staff consultation? If so, what was helpful about the consultation?
4. How did the crisis end?
5. What did staff do to help bring the crisis to an end?
6. What else did staff do that was helpful?
7. What else worked in this particular crisis situation?
8. What was learned from this incident?
9. What, if anything, should be done differently in the future?
10. What, if anything, might have prevented this particular crisis?
11. What else might be helpful in preventing future crises?

IDEAS FOR ON-CALL CRISIS MANAGEMENT

Contacting On-Call Staff

Many residential facilities use on-call or "backup" systems in which a particular RYCW, therapist, social worker, or administrative staff person is contacted in the event of an emergency. There are several reasons that such systems exist. First, they offer support to frontline staff. Next, on-call systems provide a forum for brainstorming when difficult or problematic situations arise. Third, when crisis situations occur, oftentimes there are certain decisions that agencies require those in supervisory roles to make. These might include the discharge of a youth who has broken program rules, an emergency admittance to a facility, the medical or psychiatric hospitalization of a youth, the involvement of law enforcement, and so on.

Each agency has its own policy regarding chain of command, when to call, and so forth. Again, above all else, we encourage RYCWs to follow their agencies' guidelines in this regard. In addition, when contacting the on-call person, we feel that it is important that RYCWs are clear on several accounts:

1. What is the concern for which the on-call person is being contacted? Remember to use action-based language and/or videotalk to clearly convey what the youth in question are *doing*. Remain as objective as possible, and try not to let emotions pepper descriptions.
2. What is needed from the on-call person?
3. Avoid sharing a theory about what the problem stemmed from; there really is no time for theoretical proselytizing at this juncture.
4. Discuss what hasn't worked, what may have worked in the past to any degree, and what might work in the future. This will avoid the wasted time of the on-call person possibly suggesting the same thing.
5. Before hanging up, make sure that there is absolute clarity about what is to be done.

We've seen several crises spin further out of control because the RYCW really didn't understand what he or she was expected to do next. Within a day or two, it's a good idea for RYCWs to meet personally with the on-call person for a debriefing.

When RYCWs Are On Call

In the event that an RYCW is on call, we revert to the basics of this collaborative, competency-based approach:

1. Be sure to listen to, acknowledge, and validate the RYCW or other staff that is making the contact. This can make a signifi-

cant difference to the person calling, as oftentimes staff members just need to know that they have support and are doing a good job.

2. Collaborate with the RYCWs on shift. Utilize their expertise to create change.

3. Get a clear description of what the youth in question are doing that presents a problem. Remember to get action-based descriptions.

4. Find out what the RYCWs on shift (or, if known, on other shifts as well) may have done that hasn't worked, has worked to some degree, and might work.

5. Encourage the RYCWs on duty to be creative and do something different if what they're doing isn't working.

6. Work to resolve the immediate crisis and don't be concerned with solving every problem on a unit.

Here's an example of how an on-call RYCW might work with RYCWs on shift who are experiencing a crisis:

On-call: Hello.

RYCW: Hi, Lauren. We have a situation here. One of the residents, Annie, is threatening to beat up another one, Gina. She's really pissed.

On-call: Okay. Are they separated now?

RYCW: Yeah. Annie is sitting in the kitchen. I can see her from here, and Gina is in her room.

On-call: Good thinking. It sounds like you've got things quiet for now. So what do you think we need to concentrate on most at this point?

RYCW: I'm worried that Annie's gonna just lose it and hit her.

On-call: Okay. Who else is on shift with you?

RYCW: Pam.

On-call: Have the two of you had time to talk about what you think you should do?

RYCW: Not yet.

On-call: Okay, how about if you have Pam come within hearing distance of you so that we can brainstorm.

RYCW: Okay. [Gets Pam who is keeping an eye on Annie in the kitchen]

On-call: So, how have you two managed to keep Annie from Gina so far?

RYCW: Well, Pam calmed her down.

On-call: How did she do that?

RYCW: [Asks Pam] She says that she can calm Annie down by reminding her that she's due to be discharged soon—which is one of her goals.

On-call: Great. Will that keep her calm enough to make it through the night?

RYCW: [Consults with Pam] We think so. Pam is going to talk with her some more.

On-call: Good. If we can get through the night, then there will be a better opportunity to brainstorm on what to do in the morning. And if you have any further trouble, just call me and we'll go from there. Good job!

RYCW: Thanks!

Remember to be clear on what the concern is and keep an eye on safety. Oftentimes, a goal becomes one of making it through an evening because more staff are generally available during daytime hours.

In other instances, it can be helpful for the on-call RYCW to speak directly to the youth. Here's a recent situation that Bob worked with while on call:

Bob: Hello.

RYCW: Hi, Bob. We're having some trouble with Craig. He's refusing to take his medication and he's on some pretty heavy stuff, Lithium, and it's his first night here.

Bob: Okay, what have you tried so far?

RYCW: I talked with him and so did Bill, but he still wouldn't take it. He said they changed his medication and it's not right. But we know it is.

Bob: What do you think might work with him?

RYCW: We're kinda stuck. We're not sure.

Bob: How about if you put him on the phone so I can speak with him?

RYCW: Okay. [Goes and gets Craig]

Craig: Hello.

Bob: Hi, Craig. We haven't met, but my name is Bob. Sometimes staff call me when they're trying to figure stuff out. So what's going on?

Craig: Man, they changed my medicine and didn't tell me. I'm not taking it 'cause it's wrong.

Bob: I'm sorry if your medication was changed without your knowing. You have a right to be upset. So what do you think we should do, because your medication is important?

Craig: I don't know.

Bob: What have you done in the past when your medication was changed?

Craig: Well, they changed it before, and I didn't like it.

Bob: Yeah, change can be difficult sometimes. And what did you do to get yourself to take it?

Craig: I just decided to try it.

Bob: That's great. I bet you've handled some other decisions, too, that may have seemed hard at first.

Craig: Yeah.

Bob: So it seems we're up against another decision here. What I'm wondering is how you can use all of your past expertise in making decisions right now?

Craig: That's a tough one.

Bob: It sure is. And that's why I'm wondering how you've been able to make some tough decisions before.

Craig: I guess I could try it.

Bob: Okay. So you'll try it, and then we'll talk with your caseworker tomorrow and let her know how you feel. Okay?

Craig: Okay.

Bob: Is there anything else you might want to talk about?

Craig: Not really.

Bob: Okay. Thanks, Craig. It's been great talking with you.

Again, we are working to resolve the immediate crisis. We are not trying to fix youth or do "corrective" procedures. In our experience, if we can communicate with youth in a way that fits with them we can resolve situations rather quickly. We are referring to a collaborative process between on-call staff, RYCWs on shift, and the youth involved. We begin with acknowledgment and validation and work toward resolution by being goal oriented and creative.

SMOKEY THE BEAR VERSUS FREDDY THE FIREMAN: PREVENTING CRISES BEFORE THEY HAPPEN

Periodically, we hear RYCWs say, "All I do is put out fires," referring to the phenomenon sometimes seen in residential treatment in which, over the course of one's shift, many interpersonal conflicts (youth to youth and youth to staff) appear to spontaneously combust, much like wildfire on a dry prairie. Continually putting out fires on shift can contribute to burnout among RYCWs, compel them to call in sick, and cause an RYCWs' overall level of supervision and effectiveness to deteriorate. We refer to the RYCW who is continually "putting out fires" as Freddie the Fireman. We believe that through the use of language and through collaboration with the youth in care, Freddie can transform himself or herself into Smokey the Bear, thereby preventing fires. To do this, we offer several ideas.

Acknowledgment, Validation, and Accountability

By listening to, acknowledging, and validating youth on an everyday basis, the established therapeutic relationships can provide preventive buffers for future crises. One particular method that we recommend is linking what youth are experiencing internally with that for which they are accountable by using the word "and" (Bertolino, 1999). Recall that some actions are okay and others are not. This may seem a relatively simple idea, but we have found it to be extremely effective. Here's an example of how we do this:

> **Youth:** I'm gonna get him later!
>
> **RYCW:** Matt, it's okay for you to be mad. You can be as mad as you need to and it's not okay for you to try tod hurt him.

All we want to do is acknowledge how youth feel and send a message that, although they may feel a certain way, some behaviors will not be tolerated.

Anticipating Compliance

In working with youth, we anticipate that they will comply. If youth balk, hesitate, or flat out don't agree with what we are requesting of them, we don't consider them to be *resistant* or oppositional. Instead, we reconsider what we are doing as RYCWs and work to find another way of communicating with youth that is better for them. Again, this requires RYCWs to be creative and to think "out of the box."

Using What You Already Know

Since RYCWs spend the majority of their time on shift with youth, there are many opportunities to learn what makes a difference for youth on an individual basis. For example, an RYCW may discover on shift that a particular youth is good at sports. Another youth may have information in his or her file stating that he or she has a history of being a good student. Information can also be gathered by observing youth as they interact with one another and staff. We recommend that RYCWs file these observations and learnings in their minds and share them with other staff members during residential staffings.

Information and Education, Not Confrontation

Confrontation really only works if the idea of confrontation "fits" with a youth's ideas about how he or she changes. Usually, confrontations, such as "You need to _____ or else . . ." or "You better _____," that RYCWs use to attempt to force compliance from a youth, come off as only disrespectful and invalidating. In addition, confrontational communication styles typically only escalate a youth and teach that through "power tactics" and threats, one can get others to do what he or she wants.

Although there certainly are instances when RYCWs must be directive, we have found that approaches that use *information* and *education* tend to not only be more effective but more respectful (Bertolino, 1999). By using evocation and elicitation, we establish a context whereby youth have the education and information they need to make good decisions. Here's a case example of Bob's to illustrate this idea:

During a week when he was on call, a youth at the girls' long-term facility at Bob's agency decided that she was going to run away. The RYCWs on shift contacted Bob and informed him of the situation. After a few moments of talking with the RYCWs, Bob asked to speak with the girl. He proceeded to talk with her and said, "It sounds like you've had a rough time today, and whatever you're feeling is okay. You know, from what the staff have told me, you're really smart. So I realized that you'd want to have all the information you needed before you made a final decision about whether to stay or take off. I'm just gonna say some quick things and then you'll be better prepared to make your decision. Okay, well, you probably already know this, but no one wants you to go, and we'll help you in whatever way we can. If you decide to leave, we'll be concerned about your safety because lots of things can happen to you on the run that you don't want to happen. We'll be left with no choices. We'll have to call the police and report you missing. Then when you're picked up—a day from now or a month from now—they'll take you into custody. I don't know what they'll do with you for sure after that, but my guess is that won't get you any closer to home—which I know is what you want. It may even get you put somewhere that you'll like even less than where you are now. Now you may or may not already know what I just told you, but at least I know you have the information to make a good decision. In fact, I'm confident that you'll make a good decision. Also, you can pass that information on to others who may be in similar situations, deciding what to do too."

It has been said that the best prevention is education. What we are doing is offering information to youth so that they can be empowered to make good decisions. When we use confrontation, youth perceive us as trying to control them. However, when we use information and education, youth can have the sense that they are "driving the bus." This, we believe, can help youth to save face and, ultimately, to make more informed decisions in the future.

Stories, Fairy and Folk Tales, and Metaphors

The use of stories, fairy and folk tales, and metaphors as a therapeutic technique with youth is well documented (Barker, 1985, 1996; Combs and Freedman, 1990; Gordon, 1978; Kopp, 1995; Mills and Crowley, 1986; Wallas, 1985). We know that stories captivate youth's attention and help to lead to the creation of new meanings and understandings. In turn, this can lead to new ways of viewing and doing. We see these media as an excellent way for RYCWs to connect with youth and help them to change. In addition, RYCWs can use stories with youth to

- normalize experiences,
- acknowledge realities and natural experiences,
- offer hope,
- bypass everyday conscious ways of processing information, and
- remind youth and others of previous solutions and resources (Bertolino, 1999; O'Hanlon and Bertolino, 1998).

Here is an example:

> I (B. B.) worked with a girl, Melanie, who would often become very upset in the evenings when she would think about her family. At times, this would escalate into suicidal ideation. I told her several stories over a period of three or four months, none of which seemed to make much of a difference for her. Then one day, she stopped me in the hallway of the emergency shelter and said, "I'm doing what you told me, and it makes me feel better." Confused, I asked, "What did I suggest that you do?" To this, Melanie replied, "Don't you remember? You told me a story about Laura Ingalls Wilder and how she used to journal. I tried that, and it worked." For the duration of her stay at the facility, Melanie reported no further thoughts of suicide.

Stories, tales, and metaphors draw the attention of youth. Therefore, these media can serve as very helpful tools for RYCWs during crisis situations. We also view them as an excellent preventive measure, as they can contribute to youth feeling understood, acknowledged, and supported and can help them to recall previous solutions, abilities, and resources.

Self-Disclosure

> Bob was working with a young man named Vince who used to lose his temper quickly. He told Vince that when he was younger, he would sometimes throw the bat when playing baseball when things didn't go his way. Bob learned that he had to curb that behavior if he wanted to continue to play. Several days later, an RYCW told Bob that Vince had said to him, "Did you know that Bob used to get really mad and lose his temper in sports? I'm working on my temper 'cause I don't want to get kicked outta here."

The connective tissue between RYCWs and youth in residential treatment is the relationship. RYCW self-disclosure helps to establish a common wavelength between staff and youth (Bertolino, 1999). Further, some report that self-disclosure on the part of the practitioner is one of the most important factors in treatment (Bertolino, 1998b). We see self-disclosure as a way of letting youth know that RYCWs are human and fallible. This, in and of itself, can be preventive.

UNCONDITIONAL CONVERSATIONS: THE POWER OF RELATIONSHIPS

If you ask people about their experiences growing up, most will recall at least one person whom they felt unconditionally accepted them for who they were (Bertolino, 1999). This person may have also helped them through some tough times. In this earlier publication, Bob remarked:

> Sometimes these people were family members or long-time close friends; at other times, they were only brief acquaintances. For adolescents who are experiencing trouble in their lives, a single person can make all the difference in the world.

We have heard countless stories from former clients and residents about how an RYCW has made a difference for them. As we have stressed, it is important that RYCWs consider each interaction with youth, however brief, as important. We can also tap into the media and history as a means of identifying people who might influence youth in a positive way. For example, movies, such as *The Karate Kid, Mr. Holland's Opus, Good Will Hunting, Dangerous Minds,* and others, demonstrate the power of relationships.

Given the tremendous impact of media and pop culture on society today, most youth look up to certain figures in the public eye. In a collaborative, competency-based approach, we can elicit ideas from youth about how their heroes and idols solved problems and how they might incorporate something similar into their lives. We also can tell stories about famous people who we have heard have solved problems similar to those which youth are experiencing. Next are a couple of examples of how RYCWs can use this idea. The first is with a youth who has been in trouble for fighting:

RYCW: Hey Joel, I heard you like Pearl Jam. Is that right?

Joel: Yeah.

RYCW: You know who Eddie Vedder is?

Joel: The lead singer.

RYCW: A few years ago, on MTV and in magazines, we would hear about how he was getting into a lot of fights. We don't hear too much about that these days. Why do you suppose that is?

Joel: I don't know.

RYCW: What do you suppose he's doing differently?

Joel: I guess he's thinking more.

RYCW: About what?

Joel: Not fighting—'cause he just gets thrown in jail.

RYCW: Yeah, that's a possibility. Anything else?

Joel: I'm not sure.

RYCW: I wonder if he doesn't want to be that way anymore. What do you think?

Joel: Yeah.

The following dialogue occurred between Bob and a youth who was refusing to go to school:

RYCW: Scott, remember how we used to talk college football?

Scott: Yeah.

RYCW: Well, I saw this story on ESPN the other day where Peyton Manning was talking about whether or not he was going to go pro and forgo his final year of eligibility at the University of Tennessee.

Scott: Yeah, I know. He could of got a lot of money.

RYCW: That's right. Do you know why he chose to stay in school?

Scott: No.

RYCW: Well, he said that one of the reasons was that his mother told him that he'll never have another senior year. He'll always have to work and earn money—for the rest of his life. He'll only have one chance to go through his senior year, and who knows what he might miss. You know, I thought of you when I saw that story because I wonder what you might be missing.

The connection and relationship that RYCWs make with youth is the foundation upon which all else is built. This story demonstrates this:

I (K. T.) was working at a treatment center where I worked with a resident named Paul. The night before Paul moved on to another placement, he gave me some pictures he had drawn for me. I gave him an agency T-shirt, which was the standard parting gift, and used some petty-cash money to take him out to dinner. We laughed and talked a lot, and he reminisced about the good times he had had during his stay and how I had helped him. It was bedtime when we returned. He said a final good-bye at his door and closed the door quickly before I had a chance to say anything. I stood at the closed door and heard him sobbing. The next day, he was gone.

About six months later, I received a package. In the package was the agency T-shirt that I had given Paul, on which he had written, in big letters with black magic marker, "Kevien [he spelled my name wrong], I still remember you. I miss you. Thanks for everything. Paul." I still have that T-shirt.

The connections that are formed with youth can last a lifetime. But how can RYCWs recognize those significant others who have already been influential with youth? We invite youth into conversations about those people. Here are some questions to facilitate that process:

• Whom have you met in your life who knew or knows exactly what you've been through? What does that person know about you? How has it been helpful to you to know that the person understands or understood?

- Who do you look up to? How come?
- Who has helped you through tough times? How so?
- Who do you feel you can count on? (Bertolino, 1999)

These basic questions can bring about an avalanche of information. This can lead to new avenues with possibilities for youth and possibly reveal important information for future use in crisis or in the prevention of it. In addition, this idea can be taken into the present tense by connecting youth with activities where they can meet people who will become positive influences (e.g., team sports, clubs, scouting, recovery groups, etc.).

I DIDN'T DO IT!
PROMOTING ACCOUNTABILITY

We live in an age of accountability. We want our public figures, our corporations, and our communities to take responsibility for their actions. Likewise, it is important for youth to take responsibility for their actions. Here we explore ways that RYCWs can invite youth to accountability in ways that are respectful, collaborative, and competency based.

In Chapter 5, we discussed how the attentional patterns and stories that youth and others hold can have a significant influence on problems. When working with youth, it is imperative that RYCWs be aware of stories of nonaccountability, nonchoice, and determinism. That is, sometimes youth and others will attempt to explain or justify a behavior by attributing it to a genetic, developmental, interpersonal, personality, or other propensity, therefore removing accountability. Here's an example of what we're talking about:

> **RYCW:** Hey, Derrick, what's going on? Why did you hit Mike?
>
> **Derrick:** I couldn't help it.
>
> **RYCW:** What do you mean?
>
> **Derrick:** Didn't my doctor tell you that I'm ODD [oppositional defiant disorder]?

Other times, parents will subscribe to stories of nonaccountability:

> **Parent:** He has to have his medication or he'll be too wild and out of control. He can't stay calm without it.

Or, in-house or outside helpers will offer similar stories:

> **Social Services Worker:** He's had trouble wherever he's been. Just do the best you can with him. His doctor said that he really doesn't know what he's doing a lot of the time. He's just so impulsive and can't stop himself.

Although we want to continue to acknowledge what youth experience internally, we also want to challenge those stories which stand in the way of youth accepting responsibility for what they do. In addition, we want to work to clarify, in the eyes of those associated with youth, the importance of conveying accountability. Thus, our goal is one of inviting youth and others into conversations where accountability is at the forefront. In this section, we'll offer some ways that RYCWs can go about this process.

Invitations to Accountability

As with "painting doorways in corners" and "the moving walkway," when youth convey stories of nonaccountability, there are some practical ideas that RYCWs can use to invite youth into accountability (Bertolino, 1999). The following are three ways of doing this.

Reflect Back Nonaccountability Statements
Without the Nonaccountability Part

When youth use excuses or explanations that convey nonaccountability, RYCWs repeat back those statements while dropping the nonaccountability part. Here's how to do this:

> **Youth:** He called me a name so I hit him.
>
> **RYCW:** You hit him.

Youth: She pissed me off, so I took off.

RYCW: You ran away.

Youth: He's always making me mad. That's why I kicked a hole in the wall.

RYCW: You kicked a hole in the wall.

Find Counterexamples That Indicate Choice or Accountability

A second way to invite accountability is to search for exceptions to the behavior or actions for which a youth is claiming he or she isn't accountable. RYCWs can make generalizations with this technique because it is impossible for a youth to do a negative behavior twenty-four hours a day. Here's how to do this:

Youth: I can't help it. I was abused when I was little so that's the only way I know to handle my anger.

RYCW: I'm curious though, you got angry with the unit supervisor yesterday and you didn't hit her. How did you do that?

Youth: If she makes me mad, she knows I'm gonna take off.

RYCW: How come you don't take off every time you think she's mad at you?

Youth: He's gonna flunk me anyway, so why should I do my homework?

RYCW: I must be missing something. How did you manage to get some passing grades on your homework at the beginning of the semester?

*Use the Word "and" to Link Together Internal Experience
and Accountability*

We have stressed that from this perspective, all internal experience is okay, whereas not all actions are okay. As discussed earlier in this chapter, it can be helpful to reflect back what youth are experiencing internally and to link it with that for which they are accountable. To do this, we want to use the word "and" as opposed to "but." Here are some examples:

Youth: He always makes me so mad that I hit him.

RYCW: You can be as mad as you need to be and it's not okay to hit him.

Youth: I can't help it! I just can't stop it!

RYCW: You can feel like you can't help it and you can help it and stop it.

Youth: If he wouldn't say anything to me, I wouldn't have to cuss him out.

RYCW: It's okay to feel what you feel and it's not okay to cuss him out and say mean things.

Too often, youth get the message that they shouldn't feel the way they do. This can be extremely invalidating. At the same time, there also is a tendency for youth to use statements of nonaccountability. These three simple techniques can be very useful in simultaneously diffusing emotional reactivity and promoting accountability.

PROMOTING ACCOUNTABILITY WITHIN PREESTABLISHED CONDITIONS

Common to residential placements are the use of psychiatric diagnoses and psychotropic medications. Many mental health professionals have strong opinions about both entities. In fact, it's a sort of love-hate relationship, in that some do not believe in the use of labels and medications while others contend they are absolutely necessary. The bottom line is that RYCWs must contend with these entities, as they are used in virtually every residential program. In this section, we'll offer some practical ideas that RYCWs can consider when dealing with youth who are labeled with psychiatric diagnoses and/or are on psychotropic medication.

Working with Psychiatric Diagnoses and Labels

Psychiatric terminology and diagnoses provide a universal language for mental health professionals. Such language can serve as a guide for practitioners, including RYCWs, to help determine a plan of action. Despite this, diagnoses, or labels, are stories, not truths. They are social constructions of mental health professionals and, oftentimes, "best guesses," given a cluster of symptoms or group of behaviors. Therefore, diagnoses are extremely subjective.

Although the language associated with diagnoses can provide a medium of conversation for mental health professionals, it can stigmatize youth (Sowell, 1997). A trap for RYCWs is when the youth with whom RYCWs are working become obscured by labels. We refer to this as "runaway diagnosis," wherein youth *become* their respective diagnoses. This is when RYCWs say, "Johnny *is* ADHD," instead of saying, "Johnny was diagnosed with ADHD." We want to remind RYCWs that it is important to work with the youth, not the diagnosis (Bertolino, 1999). Thus, we want to use action-based language to be clear on what youth are doing that is a problem.

As easy as it is for RYCWs to succumb to the concept of diagnosis, youth are equally vulnerable. They can become personally tied to diagnosis and use it as a way of fending off accountability. The dominant story can become "I can't help it. I have ADHD." We want to move youth away from ideas about external control and inevitability and invite accountability and internal control. We can do this by helping to attribute actions to the youth and not to their diagnoses. Based on the aforementioned methods, here are three ways that RYCWs can invite youth into conversations for accountability:

> **Youth:** I can't help it. I hit him because I have conduct disorder.
>
> **RYCW:** You hit him.
>
> **Youth:** Didn't you read my file? I'm ADHD. I can't focus.
>
> **RYCW:** I'm wondering—I noticed yesterday that you managed to complete your assignment without becoming distracted. How did you do that?

Youth: If I wasn't ODD, then I could control what I do!

RYCW: It's okay to feel like you don't have control and you can have control.

We continue to acknowledge and validate the views that youth hold without buying into stories of nonaccountability. We can then offer alternative perspectives while inviting youth into conversations for accountability. This allows for the creation of new, less oppressive, and alternative stories in which youth are empowered to act over that which is controllable in their lives.

Working with Psychotropic Medications

Psychotropic medications for the treatment of psychiatric diagnoses such as ADD/ADHD, ODD, conduct disorder, as well as many others, are being prescribed for youth at increasing rates (American Psychiatric Association, 1994). A recent review of research has called this practice into question by suggesting that such a trend is unethical, ineffective, and potentially dangerous (Fisher and Fisher, 1997). This should be a principle concern of all RYCWs because the well-being of youth must never be compromised.

If medications are prescribed for a youth in residential placement, it's important that the RYCWs become as well informed as possible. Some agencies offer training to familiarize RYCWs with medications and their side effects. In the event that RYCWs do not receive this type of training, it is still important that RYCWs find out what a medication or combination of medications are *supposed* to do, what side effects to look for, and how to monitor those side effects (Bertolino, 1999). We view medication as a viable option for some youth. By understanding what medication can and cannot do, RYCWs can move to facilitate accountability with youth.

Unfortunately, with youth, what often accompanies the prescription of psychotropic drugs is the sense that the medication itself is in charge. In a previous publication, Bob (Bertolino, 1999) wrote,

> Without the medication, the youth is "out of control" or "can't control" his or her behavior and actions. Such a message provides excuses for youth and removes personal responsibility.

As [RYCWs], it is important to continue to hold a youth accountable whether he or she is on medications or not.

To promote accountability with youth when medication therapy is involved, RYCWs can again revert to the methods offered in the beginning of this chapter. Here are some examples:

Youth: The morning shift forgot to give me my medication so I couldn't help it. I hit him.

RYCW: You hit him.

Youth: I've been taking medicine for my anger since I was really little. If I don't get it, I can't sit still.

RYCW: I'm curious. Your mom told me that she doesn't always remember to give you your medication when you're on home visits, but she also told me that recently you've been able to sit through baseball games and movies. How have you managed to sit still for so long on those weekends without your medication?

Youth: If I don't get my medication on time, I know I'll lose control.

RYCW: You can feel like you can't control yourself without your medication and you can still control yourself.

There's a fourth way of inviting youth who are on medication into accountability. What RYCWs want to do is to find out from youth what percentage of their desired behavior is due to them being "in charge" as opposed to the medication (Bertolino, 1999). Here's how to do this:

Youth: My medication calms me down so I can control myself.

RYCW: It makes you feel calmer. Is that right?

Youth: Yeah.

RYCW: So, when you feel like you're more in control, what are you doing?

Youth: I don't hit things or break things.

RYCW: How do you get yourself to do that?

Youth: I just stop myself.

RYCW: You know, I haven't come across a medication yet that makes decisions for people or actually takes control of what they do. For you, what percentage of being in control do you think is because of things you're doing, and what percentage is due to the medication?

Youth: I guess 60 percent me and 40 percent my Ritalin.

RYCW: What does that 60 percent of you do to help you make good decisions and stay in control?

Youth: I just keep telling myself that I can do it—I can stay in control.

We want to help youth to gain a sense that they are making decisions and are ultimately in control, or "driving the bus," not the medication they are taking. The medication may be affecting how they *feel*, but no medication makes decisions or controls youth. By using conversations such as the ones offered, RYCWs can promote accountability and invite and empower youth to an improved sense of personal agency.

Further Conversations on Accountability

As discussed in Chapter 4, the lives of youth in residential treatment are often shaped by level systems. In fact, youth can become quite attached to their higher levels and privileges. Oftentimes, a major focus becomes one of maintaining the current level of privileges and working to acquire more. In effect, under such systems, being accountable for actions can often lead to loss of privileges or to level demotions. Thus, many youth are reluctant to be accountable because the privileges they've accumulated are all they have. A loss of privileges can be devastating.

Experiencing the natural consequences of behavior may not only help youth to realize the possible unpleasant effects but may also allow them to see that they have some control over avoiding these consequences by behaving differently. For example, in performing a natural consequence of property damage, a youth may find that he or she is good at carpentry. Then, the RYCW can reinforce this skill as an ability or strength. Durrant (1993) noted that experiencing some personal agency or control over one's own behavior and its consequences is one of the key contributors to viewing oneself as competent.

As mentioned with other contexts, when inviting youth into conversations for accountability, RYCWs should avoid giving lectures. Often, when confronting youth, RYCWs are inclined to lecture them to wrestle a confession, or admission of accountability, out of them. It's important to separate youth from their actions and convey positive regard. Too often, youth are hesitant to be accountable because they fear the RYCW will think less of them. Accountability can always be conveyed with respect.

Chapter 8

The Journey of 1,000 Miles: Exploring Future Roads with Possibilities

A journey of 1,000 miles begins with a single step.

Lao Tzu (Chinese proverb)

As a way of tying the ideas in this book together, in this chapter we'll explore ways of "solidifying" or "anchoring" the changes that youth have made in residential placement. We'll also discuss ideas for sharing change with larger social contexts, rituals of transition, and placement discharge. Last, we'll offer some final thoughts on what we've shared throughout this book.

THE BIG PICTURE: SHARING CHANGE WITH LARGE AUDIENCES

Good news about youth (e.g., honor roll, academic achievements, sports successes, community contributions, and so on) appears in newspapers and in other media every day (Bertolino, 1999). This kind of attention can help to amplify and spread new, valued stories about youth. We believe this sharing with larger social contexts can strengthen the valued stories of youth (Freedman and Combs, 1996). Freeman, Epston, and Lobovits (1997) remarked, "The process of gathering information to share with others invites further 'performance of meaning,' thereby strengthening the narrative" (p. 125). We view this process as very important because, oftentimes, what we hear about youth is negative. Our aim is to share with large audiences what it is that youth are doing that is positive.

With youth in residential placement, when positive change, signifying accomplishment, growth, overcoming adversity, or graduation to some type of higher level, occurs we want to highlight, amplify, and share that change with others. We're not talking about media attention here. We believe that RYCWs can use other practical ways within the context of residential placement to help youth to share their accomplishments and to punctuate change. The following are three ideas that we have found particularly useful.

Collecting Evidence Through Scrapbooks, Collages, Posters, and Journals

Take a moment to ask yourself this question: "When I was growing up, did my parents/guardians keep track of my accomplishments in some way?" Many people can answer a hearty "Yes" to this question and describe scrapbooks, how papers were hung on refrigerators, and so on. In fact, happy memories are often attached to such collections and with these accomplishments being shared with others (e.g., overcoming an obstacle, winning an award, getting a good grade, graduating, etc.).

As RYCWs, we can encourage this practice. We can help youth to start scrapbooks or journals or to create collages or posters signifying change over any designated length of time or punctuating a specific, symbolic event. They can be done individually with youth or as part of an ongoing group process. These "collections of competence can then be shared with other residents, staff, or anyone the youth chooses (Bertolino, 1999). Here's how Bob often talks with youth about starting a way of tracking change:

> Down the road, others may be curious as to how you managed to get the upper hand with _____ (fill in the blank). I'm wondering, sometimes kids or teenagers have scrapbooks, diaries, or other ways of keeping track of their accomplishments. I'm curious as to how you will be keeping track of your struggle with _____ (fill in the blank). What are some ideas that might work for you?

The idea of collecting evidence of change is illustrated in a case of Bob's:

> Owen was a rather meek and shy young boy who seemed to have a difficult time getting a word in edgewise with his peers. They would often talk about themselves in ways that contributed to Owen feeling inept and unskilled. He told Bob that he wasn't good at anything. Bob suggested that he and Owen conduct an experiment to see if his view of himself was accurate. Bob suggested that the two track what he did over the course of two weeks and then review the results. Bob gave Owen a scrapbook and suggested that he enclose any "evidence" of what he was doing over the two-week period.
>
> One week later, Bob and Owen met. Owen was beaming; he had a huge grin on his face. With an air of confidence, he opened his scrapbook and said, "Look!" When Bob looked at Owen's collection of evidence, he found letters from RYCWs, assignments with high grades, and an approved level promotion. Owen continued his scrapbook and took great pride in showing the other residents his competencies.

Another possibility is to use "letters of evidence" that punctuate specific instances of change (see Figure 8.1) and/or an "evidence log" for RYCWs, staff, teachers, and others to sign off on when positive change has been identified (see Figure 8.2) (Bertolino, 1999). These can also be helpful when youth go for "home visits," as parents and legal guardians can sign off on them as well. Again, the use of such a tool can help youth and others to focus on what it is that youth are doing that's right. The long-term and ongoing effects of this process are immeasurable. By using a paper-based format, youth can keep their collections for years to come and add to them in the future if they wish.

Youth As Consultants

When youth have made positive changes, in some ways, they have developed expertise. Freeman and colleagues (1997) wrote that when a child, in their example, has taken significant steps toward revising his or her relationship with a problem, he or she

FIGURE 8.1. Letter of Evidence

OFFICIAL
LETTER OF EVIDENCE

Name: _____

Week of: _____

Type of Evidence Reviewed:

_____
_____
_____
_____
_____
_____

Verified by: _____
Date: _____

"has gained knowledge and expertise that may assist others grappling with similar concerns" (p. 126). In residential treatment, RYCWs can use the expertise of youth to help other youth. In a sense, they can become consultants to other youth who may be experiencing similar difficulties.

FIGURE 8.2. Evidence Log

MY EVIDENCE LOG

NAME: _____

WEEK OF: _____

☺ 1.

☺ 2.

☺ 3.

☺ 4.

☺ 5.

Youth As Peer Partners

Another way to share change with others is to have youth who have successfully completed a program become mentors to other youth. At the agency where Bob works, youth often become "peer partners" and work with RYCWs. These youth are trained and then spend a few hours a week offering conversation, support, companionship, and, often, invaluable ideas to youth in other residential programs (Bertolino, 1999). Such a program benefits both youth who have experienced positive change and those in search of it.

CERTIFIABLY CHANGED

To signify and solidify change in regard to a problem or in the area of a problem, the use of certificates can be especially symbolic. Again, if one thinks about his or her past, sometimes memories of receiving awards and certificates can be recalled. For example, if a youth wins a spelling bee, he or she gets a certificate. The same may hold true for having good attendance. Certificates can be awarded for overcoming specific or general problems. We also see the awarding of certificates as a way of strengthening the relationships between youth and residential care staff.

In residential placement, RYCWs can award certificates for any number of accomplishments. For example, a youth might be given a certificate for overcoming temper tantrums. Also, a certificate might be awarded for standing up to or opposing male violence. Certificates are very easy to create. Bob does them on his home computer with the use of a word processing program. Figures 8.3 and 8.4 offer some examples of certificates that can be used in residential settings.

AT EVERY ENDING IS A NEW BEGINNING: DISCHARGE AS TRANSITION

Most residential programs are merely points of transition for youth. That is, youth transition in and out of programs in an ongoing manner. With this in mind, and from a collaborative, competency-based perspective, from the moment a youth enters a program, preparation is made for his or her discharge. Yet, as RYCWs prepare youth for discharge from a program, there are some specific points to consider. We will outline a few of these here.

FIGURE 8.3. Tantrum Tamer Certificate

Tantrum Tamer

Certificate

This certificate is hereby awarded to

Kelly Smith

On this day, December 3rd, 1999
For demonstrating her ability to tame tantrums

Scott Davis
Scott Davis, RYCW

Preparatory Questions

As discharge nears, RYCWs can encourage youth to think about several questions that build on the successes they have experienced. Some questions serve to identify and amplify change, others inquire about possible roadblocks, and still others focus on the future.

FIGURE 8.4. Certificate of Change

Certificate of Change

This certificate is hereby awarded to

Shane Williams

On this day, December 3rd*, 1999*
For success in standing up to juvenile delinquency
And
Getting his life back

Lisa Meyers
Lisa Meyers, RYCW

Identifying and Amplifying Change

- What specifically have you learned while here that will help you wherever you go?
- How is what you've accomplished in this program going to help you when you go back home or to another placement?
- In what ways do you feel you are different from the way you were when you first came here? How can that help you down the road?

Possible Roadblocks

- What might come up over the next few days/weeks/months that might present a challenge to your staying on track?

- Is there anything that might happen in the near future that might pose a threat to all the changes you've made?
- Since you've learned new ways of doing things, how will you handle things differently than before when you encounter difficulties?

Focusing on the Future

- What will you be doing in the future to keep things going in the right direction?
- How will you be keeping things moving forward?
- How can others be of help to you in staying on track down the road?

In preparing youth for discharge, we don't tell them that they will encounter difficulty. We only suggest that everyone experiences adversity from time to time and that there *might* be roadblocks to negotiate along the way. With that said, should a youth encounter difficulty, he or she can be better prepared to deal with things differently than before.

Celebrating the Discharge

Many times when a youth is discharged from a facility, there is a celebration. Sometimes staff members will come in on their off time to say good-bye. We feel it is very important for those staff members who have made an impact on the life of the departing youth, or who have been impacted by the departing youth, to have some semblance of closure. Such a process can be meaningful to both the staff and the youth.

The proceedings should highlight the changes in, and competencies of, the departing youth. Sometimes, a youth's peers are each asked to say something about the success of the departing youth or give words of encouragement to him or her. Another possibility is to allow the departing youth the opportunity to share with others in the program (including staff) how he or she successfully completed the program, highlighting along the way those people and things that helped him or her. Through this process, other youth may find something in the departing youth's presentation that they can apply to themselves. The key is to be creative and to instill a sense of hope for continued success in the future.

Discharge Rituals

One symbolic and often powerful way to mark the transition is the discharge ritual. This is a way of declaring the new status of a youth and making it public so that he or she may be seen in a new light. It marks a change for the youth and allows for the consolidation of his or her new self-view. Oftentimes, this process involves symbolic gifts or trophies or, as discussed earlier, a certificate (Durrant, 1993).

Involving the departing youth in the design of his or her ritual can be effective and is respectful. Youth sometimes identify ceremonies that would be meaningful to them or methods of closure that they desire. If involving the youth is not an option, we feel it is still imperative to individualize the ritual to the particular youth in a way that celebrates his or her strengths, resources, and abilities and that acknowledges and validates the changes he or she has made. This creates a context in which to transition these qualities into his or her new environment:

> Kevin recalls the discharge of Jack, a twelve-year-old, from one of the facilities at which he worked. When staff would catch Jack "doing something right" or making an effort to change his behavior, they would ask him how he did it. With a sly grin, his standard first answer was, "It's magic." Jack was always fascinated with card tricks and disappearing acts. On the day Jack was transitioned out of the facility, the treatment team presented him with a beginner magician's kit to symbolize his gift of being able to "magically" change his behavior.

Discharge rituals can be helpful for those youth who are leaving the facility on less than positive terms as well. These types of rituals frame the discharge not as a failure but as a change and put a more positive spin on it. The idea is not to have the youth feeling like a failure when he or she leaves, but to have him or her feeling as though the next placement will be a new step. Durrant (1993) gives the following example:

> A girl who had a propensity for running away asked to leave the facility where she was staying. Her leaving was placed within a positive frame and the various successes she had achieved were highlighted as reason to be hopeful that she would not continue running away. Her leaving was framed as a considered decision, rather than a fleeing one. The residential staff gave her a magnet with a sneaker on it, so that wherever she went she could display it prominently to remind her that they had seen her on many occasions facing conflict and problems. Their aim was to give her something that symbolized this leaving as different to previous ones. It signified the beginning of a different future. (p. 177)

DON'T FORGET ME! THE LIGHT THAT NEVER GOES OUT

Many youth, for one reason or another, find themselves shuffling in and out of a multitude of placements over the course of months or years. We refer to this as the "shelter shuffle." We liken the effect to what it might have been like if, when you were a child, you and your family moved to a different city every few months or so—the experience of having to introduce yourself to a new set of other people repeatedly and of having to adjust to new surroundings and routines just when you were getting used to the old. Often, this can be a very traumatizing and humiliating experience. Many crises arise in residential placement as a direct result of a youth doing the shelter shuffle, and rehearsing and enacting internal narratives of rejection, instability, and anger.

As RYCWs, we simply want to be sensitive to the fact that many youth will experience the shelter shuffle. They will have little sense of being grounded or having any permanent, or at least stable, "roots." To counter this, we continue to value the relationships that are created, to listen, to acknowledge, and to validate. But, we also "leave the light on."

Hillary Rodham Clinton once wrote, "It takes a village to raise a child" (Clinton, 1996). We echo this sentiment and amplify it in regard to youth experiencing residential placement. In fact, we would say that, as RYCWs, once we come into contact with a youth, that relationship continues indefinitely—each story continues to evolve. Our impact extends beyond the walls within which we work.

We are greatly pained when we hear stories of RYCWs and other staff who are told to never associate with youth once they have left placement, or of RYCWs who want nothing to do with youth once they have been discharged. This is truly disappointing. The process of supporting and strengthening youth and their families and being available to help is ongoing. Although we view residential placement as a transitioning point for youth, we must always remember that their struggles to survive are an everyday issue.

Whenever we have youth contact us after placement, we consider it a gift. Why? It tells us that they trust us to help them in whatever ways we can. Oddly, most often this means just listening to them. We can make a promise to each RYCW who utilizes the ideas in this book—you will have youth contact you after placement. The question each RYCW will have to answer is "What will I do?"

During a workshop presentation, a participant told Bob a quote that has stuck with him: "Children and youth do not fall through the cracks. They fall through people's fingers." We suggest that RYCWs close the spaces between their fingers and continue to help when called upon. It can be said that the response of RYCWs to youth throughout placement and *in the future* will play a part in their growth. It's simply up to each RYCW to do his or her part in the raising of each youth. So, we recommend "keeping the light on."

COUNTERING BURNOUT AND VALUING YOURSELF

In our jobs as RYCWs, we have encountered countless dedicated fellow RYCWs. These folks are eager to "do what it takes" to be as effective as possible. With such dedication and eagerness can come high levels of stress because residential treatment brings with it many pitfalls that are common to the helping professions, as well as many that are unforeseen. However, RYCWs must also contend with something else—theoretical approaches. When we combine the everyday happenings of residential treatment with theoretical approaches that only are pathology or problem focused, over time, it can become very disheartening and lead to a sense of hopelessness. For RYCWs, such feelings can lead to burnout.

The collaborative, competency-based approach we have outlined in this book takes a different view. Instead of continually letting our theories tell us what can't be done, we focus on what's possible and what's changeable. We don't ignore the realities that youth face, we acknowledge and attend to them, while simultaneously asking, "What's right?" Such a focus, we believe, can breathe new life into views and create optimism that theories often drain from RYCWs. This, in turn, can counter RYCW burnout.

At the heart of residential placement is the RYCW. It is impossible to overstate the impact that RYCWs have each day in their interactions with youth. We hope that as an RYCW you will be reminded of this and value yourself. The work of RYCWs, with the youth of yesterday, today, and tomorrow, is as important and valuable as any other kind of work on this planet.

References

Adler, J. (Ed.) (1981). *Fundamentals of group child care: A textbook and instructional guide for child care workers.* Cambridge, MA: Balinger Publishing Company.

Allport, G. (1961). *Patterns and growth in personality.* New York: Holt, Rinehart, and Winston.

American Psychiatric Association (1994). *Diagnostic and statistical manual of mental disorders* (Fourth edition). Washington, DC: American Psychiatric Association.

Andersen, T. (Ed.) (1991). *The reflecting team: Dialogues and dialogues about the dialogues.* New York: Norton.

Anderson, H. (1997). *Conversation, language, and possibilities: A postmodern approach to therapy.* New York: Basic Books.

Arieli, M. (1997). *The occupational experience of residential child and youth care workers: Caring and its discontents.* Binghamton, NY: The Haworth Press.

Bandler, R. and Grinder, J. (1975). *Patterns of the hypnotic techniques of Milton H. Erickson, MD,* Volume I. Capitola, CA: Meta Publications.

Barker, P. (1985). *Using metaphors in psychotherapy.* New York: Brunner/Mazel.

Barker, P. (1996). *Psychotherapeutic metaphors: A guide to theory and practice.* New York: Brunner/Mazel.

Berg, I. K. (1994). *Family based services: A solution-focused approach.* New York: Norton.

Berg, I. K. and de Shazer, S. (1993). Making numbers talk: Language in therapy. In S. Friedman (Ed.), *The new language of change: Constructive collaboration in psychotherapy* (pp. 5-24). New York: Guilford.

Berg, I. K. and Gallagher, D. (1991). Solution-focused brief treatment with adolescent substance abusers. In T. C. Todd and M. D. Selekman (Eds.), *Family therapy approaches with adolescent substance abusers* (pp. 93-111). Needham Heights, MA: Allyn and Bacon.

Berg, I. K. and Miller, S. D. (1992). *Working with the problem drinker: A solution-focused approach.* New York: Norton.

Berger, P. L. and Luckmann, T. (1966). *The social construction of reality: A treatise in the sociology of knowledge.* New York: Doubleday/Anchor Books.

Bertolino, B. (1998a). Rewriting youth stories: An activity with troubled youth. In L. Hecker and S. Deacon (Eds.), *The therapist's notebook: Homework, handouts, and activities for use in psychotherapy* (pp. 391-400). Binghamton, NY: The Haworth Press.

Bertolino, B. (1998b). An exploration of change: Investigating the experiences of psychotherapy trainees. Unpublished doctoral dissertation, St. Louis University.

171

Bertolino, B. (1999). *Therapy with troubled teenagers: Rewriting young lives in progress.* New York: Wiley.

Bertolino, B. and O'Hanlon, B. (1998). *Invitation to possibility-land: An intensive teaching seminar with Bill O'Hanlon.* Bristol, PA: Brunner/Mazel.

Bobele, M., Gardner, G., and Biever, J. (1995). Supervision as social construction. *Journal of Systemic Therapies, 14*(2), 14-25.

Booker, J. and Blymer, D. (1994). Solution-oriented brief residential treatment with "chronic mental patients." *Journal of Systemic Therapies, 13*(4), 53-69.

Clinton, H. R. (1996). *It takes a village: And other lessons children teach us.* New York: Simon and Schuster.

Combs, G. and Freedman, J. (1990). *Symbol, story, and ceremony: Using metaphor in individual and family therapy.* New York: Norton.

Crone, J. E. (1984). *Getting started as a residential child care worker: A guide for beginners.* New York: Child Welfare League of America.

de Shazer, S. (1985). *Keys to solution in brief therapy.* New York: Norton.

de Shazer, S. (1988). *Clues: Investigating solutions in brief therapy.* New York: Norton.

de Shazer, S. (1991). *Putting difference to work.* New York: Norton.

de Shazer, S. (1994). *Words were originally magic.* New York: Norton.

Duncan, B. L., Hubble, M. A., and Miller, S. D. (1997). Stepping off the throne. *Family Therapy Networker, 21*(5), 22-31, 33.

Durkin, R. (1990). Competency, relevance, and empowerment: A case for restructuring of children's programs. In J. P. Anglin, C. J. Denholm, R. V. Ferguson, and A. R. Pence (Eds.), *Perspectives in professional child and youth care* (pp. 105-117). Binghamton, NY: The Haworth Press.

Durrant, M. (1993). *Residential treatment: A cooperative, competency-based approach to therapy and program design.* New York: Norton.

Durrant, M. (1995). *Creative strategies for school problems: Solutions for psychologists and teachers.* New York: Norton.

Efran, J. and Lukens, M. D. (1985). The world according to Humberto Maturana. *Family Therapy Networker, 9*(3), 23-25, 27-28, 72-75.

Epston, D. (1997). "I am a bear": Discovering discoveries. In C. Smith and D. Nylund (Eds.), *Narrative therapies with children and adolescents* (pp. 53-70). New York: Guilford.

Erickson, M. H. (1954). Special techniques of brief hypnotherapy. *Journal of Clinical and Experiential Hypnosis, 2,* 109-129.

Eron, J. B. and Lund, T. W. (1996). *Narrative solutions in brief therapy.* New York: Guilford.

Fisher, R. and Fisher, S. (1997). Are we justified in treating children with psychotropic drugs? In S. Fisher and R. Greenberg (Eds.), *From placebo to panacea: Putting drugs to the test.* New York: Wiley.

Freedman, J. and Combs, G. (1996). *Narrative therapy: The social construction of preferred realities.* New York: Norton.

Freeman, J., Epston, D., and Lobovits, D. (1997). *Playful approaches to serious problems: Narrative therapy with children and their families.* New York: Norton.

Friedman, S. (1993). *The new language of change: Constructive collaboration in psychotherapy.* New York: Guilford.

Furman, B. and Ahola, T. (1992). *Solution talk: Hosting therapeutic conversations.* New York: Norton.

Gentle Spaces News (1995). Let there be peace. In J. Canfield and M. V. Hansen (Eds.), *A 2nd helping of chicken soup for the soul: 101 more stories to open the heart and rekindle the spirit* (pp. 297-298). Deerfield Beach, FL: Health Communications.

Gordon, D. (1978). *Therapeutic metaphors: Helping others through the looking glass.* Cupertino, CA: Meta Publications.

Grinder, J., DeLozier, J., and Bandler, R. (1977). *Patterns of the hypnotic techniques of Milton H. Erickson, MD,* Volume 2. Cupertino, CA: Meta Publications.

Herman, J. L. (1992). *Trauma and recovery: The aftermath of violence—From domestic abuse to political terror.* New York: Basic Books.

Higgins, G. O. (1994). *Resilient adults: Overcoming a cruel past.* San Francisco, CA: Jossey-Bass.

Hoffman, L. (1990). Constructing realities: An art of lenses. *Family Process, 29,* 1-12.

Hoffman, L. (1993). *Exchanging voices: A collaborative approach to family therapy.* London: Karnac.

Hoyt, M. (1994). *Constructive therapies.* New York: Guilford.

Hudson, P. O. and O'Hanlon, W. H. (1991). *Rewriting love stories: Brief marital therapy.* New York: Norton.

Johnson, C. (1955). *Harold and the purple crayon.* New York: HarperCollins.

Kopp, R. R. (1995). *Metaphor therapy: Using client-generated metaphors in psychotherapy.* New York: Brunner/Mazel.

Krueger, M. A. (1990). Promoting professional teamwork. In J. P. Anglin, C. J. Denholm, R. V. Ferguson, and A. R. Pence (Eds.), *Perspectives in professional child and youth care* (pp. 123-130). Binghamton, NY: The Haworth Press.

Lambert, M. J. (1992). Implications of outcome research for psychotherapy integration. In J. C. Norcross and M. R. Goldfried (Eds.), *Handbook of psychotherapy integration* (pp. 94-129). New York: Basic Books.

Lawson, A., McElheran, N., and Slive, A. (1997). Single session walk-in therapy: A model for the 21st century. *Family Therapy News, 30*(4), 15, 25.

Levine, M. and Levine, A. (1970). *A social history of helping services: Clinic, court, school, and community.* New York: Appleton-Century-Crofts.

Lipchik, E. (1988). Purposeful sequences for beginning the solution-focused interview. In E. Lipchik (Ed.), *Interviewing* (pp. 105-116). Rockville, MD: Aspen.

Mayer, M. F., Richman, L. H., and Blacerzak, E. A. (1978). *Group care of children: Crossroads and transitions* (Second edition). New York: Child Welfare League of America.

McBride, J. (1997). *Steven Spielberg: A biography.* New York: Simon and Schuster.

Metcalf, L. (1995). *Counseling toward solutions: A practical solution-focused program for working with students, teachers, and parents.* New York: Center for Applied Research in Education.

Miller, S. D., Duncan, B. L., and Hubble, M. A. (1997). *Escape from Babel: Toward a unifying language for psychotherapy practice.* New York: Norton.

Miller, S. D., Hubble, M. A., and Duncan, B. L. (1995). No more bells and whistles. *Family Therapy Networker, 19*(2), 53-58. 62-63.

Mills, J. C. and Crowley, R. J. (1986). *Therapeutic metaphors for children and the child within.* New York: Brunner/Mazel.

Nylund, D. and Corsiglia, V. (1994). Attention to the deficits in attention-deficit disorder: Deconstructing the diagnosis and bringing forth children's special abilities. *Journal of Collaborative Therapies, 2*(2), 7-17.

O'Hanlon, B. (1982). Strategic pattern intervention: An integration of individual and family therapies based on the work of Milton H. Erickson. *Journal of Strategic and Systemic Therapies, 1*(4), 26-33.

O'Hanlon, B. (1994). The third wave. *Family Therapy Networker, 18*(6), 18-26, 28-29.

O'Hanlon, B. (1996a). Action, stories, and experience. In B. O'Hanlon, *The handout book: Complete handouts from the workshops of Bill O'Hanlon* (p. 97). Omaha, NE: Possibility Press.

O'Hanlon, B. (1996b). Acknowledgment and possibility in interviewing. In B. O'Hanlon, *The handout book: Complete handouts from the workshops of Bill O'Hanlon* (p. 1). Omaha, NE: Possibility Press.

O'Hanlon, B. (1996c). Assessment questions. In B. O'Hanlon, *The handout book: Complete handouts from the workshops of Bill O'Hanlon* (p. 3). Omaha, NE: Possibility Press.

O'Hanlon, B. and Beadle, S. (1994). *A field guide to possibilityland: Possibility therapy methods.* Omaha, NE: Possibility Press.

O'Hanlon, B. and Bertolino, B. (1998). *Even from a broken web: Brief, respectful solution-oriented therapy for sexual abuse and trauma.* New York: Wiley.

O'Hanlon, B. and Wilk, J. (1987). *Shifting contexts: The generation of effective psychotherapy.* New York: Guilford.

O'Hanlon, S. and O'Hanlon, B. (1999). Possibility therapy with families. In S. O'Hanlon and B. Bertolino (Eds.), *Evolving possibilities: The selected papers of Bill O'Hanlon.* Bristol, PA: Brunner/Mazel.

O'Hanlon, W. H. (1987). *Taproots: Underlying principles of Milton Erickson's therapy and hypnosis.* New York: Norton.

O'Hanlon, W. (1998). Possibility therapy: An inclusive, collaborative, solution-based model of psychotherapy. In M. F. Hoyt (Ed.), *The handbook of constructive therapies: Innovative approaches from leading practitioners* (pp. 137-158). San Francisco, CA: Jossey-Bass.

O'Hanlon, W. H. and Weiner-Davis, M. (1989). *In search of solutions: A new direction in psychotherapy.* New York: Norton.

Parry, A. and Doan, R. E. (1994). *Story re-visions: Narrative therapy in the postmodern world.* New York: Guilford.

Penn, P. and Sheinberg, M. (1991). Stories and conversations. *Journal of Strategic and Systemic Therapies, 10*, 30-37.

Rogers, C. R. (1951). *Client-centered therapy.* Boston, MA: Houghton-Mifflin.

Rogers, C. R. (1961). *On becoming a person: A therapist's view of psychotherapy.* Boston, MA: Houghton-Mifflin.

Rossi, E. L. (Ed.) (1980). *The collected papers of Milton H. Erickson on hypnosis* (Volumes I-IV). New York: Irvington.

Rossi, E. L., Ryan, M. O., and Sharp, F. A. (Eds.) (1983). *The seminars, workshops, and lectures of Milton H. Erickson* (Volumes I-IV). New York: Irvington.

Rowan, T. and O'Hanlon, B. (1998). *Solution-oriented therapy for chronic and severe mental illness.* New York: Wiley.

Rutter, M. (1987). Psychosocial resilience and protective mechanisms. 1987 meeting of the American Orthopsychiatric Association. *American Journal of Orthopsychiatry, 57*(3), 316-331.

Saleeby, D. (1994). Culture, theory, and narrative: The intersection of meanings in practice. *Social Work, 39*, 351-359.

Selekman, M. D. (1993). *Pathways to change: Brief therapy solutions with difficult adolescents.* New York: Guilford.

Selekman, M. D. (1997). *Solution-focused therapy with children: Harnessing family strengths for systemic change.* New York: Guilford.

Smith, C. (1997). Introduction: Comparing traditional therapies with narrative approaches. In C. Smith and D. Nylund (Eds.), *Narrative therapies with children and adolescents* (pp. 1-52). New York: Guilford.

Smith, C. and Nylund, D. (Eds.) (1997). *Narrative therapies with children and adolescents.* New York: Guilford.

Sowell, T. (1997). Dangerous labels. *Forbes,* September 22, 283.

Stein, J. A. (1995). *Residential treatment of adolescents and children: Issues, principles, and techniques.* Chicago: Nelson Hall, Inc.

Thomas, B. (1994). *Walt Disney: An American original.* New York: Hyperion.

Tiffin, S. (1982). *In whose best interest: Child welfare reform in the progressive era.* Westport, CT: Greenwood Press.

Wallas, L. (1985). *Stories for the third ear: Using hypnosis fables in psychotherapy.* New York: Norton.

Waters, D. B. and Lawrence, E. C. (1993). *Competence, courage, and change: An approach to family therapy.* New York: Norton.

White, M. and Epston, D. (1990). *Narrative means to therapeutic ends.* New York: Norton.

Wolin, S. J. and Wolin, S. (1993). *The resilient self: How survivors of troubled families rise above adversity.* New York: Villard Books.

Zeig, J. K. (Ed.) (1980). *A teaching seminar with Milton H. Erickson.* New York: Brunner/Mazel.

Zimmerman, J. and Dickerson, V. (1996). *If problems talked: Narrative therapy in action.* New York: Guilford.

Index

Change *(continued)*
  identifying, 53-54, 123-125, 126,
      164
  and language, 19, 26-27, 39
  time requirement, 13
  tracking, 157-159
Choice, 95, 150. *See also*
      Accountability
Chores, 113
Clinton, Hillary Rodham, 167-168
Cocreation, 10-11, 101-107
Collaboration
  with co-workers, 130
  in crises, 140
  with youth, 9-10, 11, 22, 24-27
Combs, G., 143, 157
Community meetings, 76-81
Competency
  assumptions, 8-14, 25-26
  contexts of, 119-120
  as focus, 4-5
  and past ability, 91
  and personal agency, 156
  of staff members, 64-65
Compliance, 141
Confrontation, 142-143
Consequences, 132, 155-156
Constructs, 127
Context, 11-12, 15, 121-123, 142
Continuity, 73
Control, 155-156
Conversations
  about past success, 45-47
  for accountability, 149-156
  competency-based, 21-27
  and doorways in corners, 37-39
  in group unit meetings, 78-79
  unconditional, 145-148
Coping, 120-121
Corsiglia, V., 92
Counseling experience, 49
Counterevidence, 90-92
Co-workers, 130. *See also* Meetings;
      Negativity; Residential
      workers; Shift change

Creativity, 114-115, 141. *See also*
      Cocreation
Crises
  and body language, 131
  de-escalation techniques, 131-133
  definition, 129
  prevention methods, 133-134,
      140-145
  and safety, 130, 138
  and shelter shuffle, 167
  and staff members, 134-140
Crone, J. E., 72, 129
Crowley, R. J., 143
Crystal ball, 102-103
Cultural idols, 145-148

DeLozier, J., 109
de Shazer, S., 47, 66-67, 103-104
Demotions, 81-83
Depression, 122
Diagnoses, psychiatric, 94, 151-153
Dickerson, V., 92
Discharge, 163-167
Disneyland, 18, 29
Doan, R. E., 10
Doorways, painting, 36-41
Drawing, 102-103, 106
Duncan, B. L., 9, 33, 35
Durkin, R., 4
Durrant, Michael
  on assessment, 43
  on crises, 130
  on discharge, 166, 167
  on feelings, 127
  on focus of care, 3-4, 13-14
  on level systems, 81, 82
  on personal agency, 156
  on shift change, 76

Education, 142-143
Efran, J., 10, 29
Empathy, 36-37
Empowerment, 126, 127

Order Your Own Copy of
This Important Book for Your Personal Library!

THE RESIDENTIAL YOUTH CARE WORKER IN ACTION
A Collaborative, Competency-Based Approach

_____ in hardbound at $39.95 (ISBN: 0-7890-0701-0)

_____ in softbound at $24.95 (ISBN: 0-7890-0912-9)

COST OF BOOKS_____

OUTSIDE USA/CANADA/
MEXICO: ADD 20%_____

POSTAGE & HANDLING_____
*(US: $3.00 for first book & $1.25
for each additional book)
Outside US: $4.75 for first book
& $1.75 for each additional book)*

SUBTOTAL_____

IN CANADA: ADD 7% GST_____

STATE TAX_____
*(NY, OH & MN residents, please
add appropriate local sales tax)*

FINAL TOTAL_____
*(If paying in Canadian funds,
convert using the current
exchange rate. UNESCO
coupons welcome.)*

☐ **BILL ME LATER:** ($5 service charge will be added)
(Bill-me option is good on US/Canada/Mexico orders only;
not good to jobbers, wholesalers, or subscription agencies.)

☐ Check here if billing address is different from
shipping address and attach purchase order and
billing address information.

Signature_____

☐ **PAYMENT ENCLOSED: $**_____

☐ **PLEASE CHARGE TO MY CREDIT CARD.**

☐ Visa   ☐ MasterCard   ☐ AmEx   ☐ Discover
☐ Diners Club
Account #_____

Exp. Date_____

Signature_____

Prices in US dollars and subject to change without notice.

NAME_____

INSTITUTION_____

ADDRESS_____

CITY_____

STATE/ZIP_____

COUNTRY_____ COUNTY (NY residents only)_____

TEL_____ FAX_____

E-MAIL_____
May we use your e-mail address for confirmations and other types of information? ☐ Yes   ☐ No

Order From Your Local Bookstore or Directly From
The Haworth Press, Inc.
10 Alice Street, Binghamton, New York 13904-1580 • USA
TELEPHONE: 1-800-HAWORTH (1-800-429-6784) / Outside US/Canada: (607) 722-5857
FAX: 1-800-895-0582 / Outside US/Canada: (607) 772-6362
E-mail: getinfo@haworthpressinc.com
PLEASE PHOTOCOPY THIS FORM FOR YOUR PERSONAL USE.

BOF96